# IN NO STRANGE LAND

# IN NO STRANGE LAND

## Some American Catholic Converts

BY

KATHERINE BURTON

*Author of "Sorrow Built a Bridge"*
*"Paradise Planters"*
*"His Dear Persuasion"*

LONGMANS, GREEN AND CO.

NEW YORK · TORONTO

1942

IN NO STRANGE LAND

248.242

2

To Robert Sargent Shriver
as a small tribute to
his mighty work of years
in the cause of converts
to the Church

# INTRODUCTION

In this book have been gathered together the brief biographies of some of the more outstanding American converts to the Catholic faith during the nineteenth century, although a few of them properly belong to our own twentieth. The earlier ones came into the Church at a time when it was almost heroic for an American to do so, a time when the flowering of New England may have seemed fair in the eyes of many, but when the growth of the Catholic Church was regarded as the spread of a noisome weed, one that should be uprooted if American culture and philosophy were to flourish. Nevertheless there were here and there a few who, with eyes opened by faith, recognized the despised weed as the Rose of the World. To them the Church presented a visage perhaps faded and worn but with the precious antiquity of an old book or painting which needed only to be freed of dust for the masterpiece to appear.

There are also mentioned here a few converts who came into the Church when conversions to Rome were becoming more common. But each of them is part of the Protestant tradition, either of New England or Virginia, or of the Mid-West. Each by teaching and training was deeply imbued with Protestantism and each bore the imprint of the American tradition of democracy.

In dealing with what may broadly be called the Concord School, writers have generally neglected or been in

ignorance of the most important reasons for the existence
of that group and of its effect on succeeding generations.
When Van Wyck Brooks' *Flowering of New England*
appeared, Henry Commager, reviewing it in the New
York *Times*, complained, even while praising it, that the
story lacked "a focus, a philosophy, a moral."   The weak-
est part of the narrative, he said, was that which described
Brook Farm and the Boston and Concord reformers without revealing first the philosophy "which furnished the
logic and moral of their lives."

Mr. Brooks' later book, *New England : Indian Summer*, was also reviewed in the *Times*, and again complaint
was made that it contained no mention of the logical and
moral factor in the formation of these people.   It was,
of course, merely the Christian faith, for all of them the
accepted basis of living.   They were thoroughly impreg-
nated with religion when they were young, and many of
them had been or remained ministers of the gospel.   Mr.
Brooks has no interest in old-fashioned religion, and
merely ignores it.   In dealing with the lives of the men
and women of that day, to him, as to Odell Shepherd,
whose literary work has taken fire from Mr. Brooks' vivid
style, religion is of no importance.   They prefer to call it
philosophy.   When Mr. Brooks speaks about religion it
is likely to be in the form of an anecdote, gently told but
with a little hidden chuckle between the lines, as when
he recounts how Emerson's uncle told the Lord he had to
get in his hay and it must not rain until he did.   Emerson's uncle meant it.   Mr. Brooks thinks it is humorous.

There was nothing amusing about religion to these people.   It is true that one by one they left their churches and sought elsewhere for a faith.   And, since they were merely groping and not sure of their goal, many of them never found any actual faith again.   They were incurably religious, but they fled the cold harshness of the Calvinism in which they had been reared, and the pale Unitarianism they took up later was not enough for the best of them.   They were people who wanted to help the poor and the untaught of their land as well as those who set in pews before them waiting to hear words they already knew, words that would never stir them from their satisfied calm to a realization of poverty and pain, of the injustice of working conditions, of the inequality of educational opportunities.

The great names that have come down to us from that era are of those who were, each in his or her way, seekers of faith and justice in the world.   And the saddest part of their history is that so few of these earnest seekers found the object of their quest.   They left the coldness of Calvinism to find a new faith that would embody not only the love of God but also the love of man.   They were to some extent still Christians, in a broad, vague way, but they were groping past the harshness in the Old Testament — the law of a tooth for a tooth — to the love, mercy and forgiveness of the New Testament.

So, Bronson Alcott had a bust of Christ in his schoolroom, and when a question of morals arose the class considered how Jesus would have answered it.   Thoreau's

writings are pervaded with a realization of the necessity
of faith, even though such a faith would be definitely one
of his own brand.    Emerson sought all his life, in East
and West, for a religion — a loving faith, not a laborious
adaptation of the one he had been trained to preach.    He
saw clearly, after his years at the Divinity School, how his
sect had become a cut and dried body with no actual life,
"a praying by the job," as George Ripley put it.    The
young ministers were taught to go out into the world with
a message, but all too soon the best of them realized they
were not preaching the humanity and the kindness of the
gospels.

There was one faith and only one which could have
satisfied their seeking, and but a few found it.    Yet nearly
every man among them was at some time or other moved
by Catholicism.    Hawthorne, we know, very strongly so,
as *The Marble Faun* shows.    Emerson often too, despite
his bitter words about the Church.    He had gone to Baltimore one day and attended Mass at the cathedral.    Back
in Concord he was much excited about it.    "There," he
told them, "is the way religion should be — the priest
and the people are nothing and the fact is everything."
When his niece wanted to become a Catholic, he told her
relatives to let her, saying that if she could find warmth
in another faith they should let her leave cold Protestantism and be a part of a vital church — "Masses, madonna
and all !"    Longfellow's verses are full of Catholicity and
the flaming humanitarianism of Holmes and Whittier
breathes its spirit.    Brownson was working his persistent

way to Catholicism through various sects, and young Isaac
Hecker was reaching the same goal.

But few of the group ever thought seriously about becoming Catholics.   For one thing they did not realize
that their own humanitarianism was but a part of that
faith.   They had escaped a harsh faith that was creedal
and it had filled them with a distrust of creeds; they
wanted to "walk past the ruin of temples to God in the
human heart."   When Ripley said what he wanted was
to call Christ "Brother," Emerson immediately inter-
posed, "Brother, yes, but never Lord."

Then, too, there was nothing to attract these products
of Harvard and of the intellectual restraint of the Puritans
in the Catholicism they saw about them.   The priests in
the small New England towns were not the type with
whom they could enter into discussions.   The missions
into which they looked now and then were shabby little
buildings with cheap statues and gaudy pictures; the people who attended them were poor folk with little appreciation of the finer arts — laborers on the railroads, diggers
of ditches and domestic servants.

The New England intellectuals knew this was not all
of Catholicism, of course, but to most of them it was its
present actuality.   It had degenerated, they thought, into
the superstitions of an illiterate group, ruled but not educated by men in other lands.   The true Catholicism for
them was preserved in music and sculpture and paintings
in old museums and in churches which were almost museums.   Emerson sent Hawthorne a copy of the "Trans-

figuration" as a gift for his new house, but it was art to them both, perhaps even allegory and a symbol, but not living fact.

Even though they saw crowded congregations of un-lettered immigrants filling the Catholic churches, even though the priests in small towns could give no time to fine talk and letters, these men could have found dignity and beauty in some of the Catholic churches had they tried. In Baltimore there were many fine churches. In New York there was more than one, among them notably the Paulist Church built by Isaac Hecker and his group of converts, all educated men. A captain from West Point, a son of the Chancellor of New York, the grandson of a lawyer who was known as the American Blackstone, were among his associates and helpers.

There was no one to tell this group of men and women the glowing truth, but it is interesting to reflect on what a difference there might have been in the religious progress in America had they become Catholic. Here and there a brave man or woman pushed through to reality, but by the time these could have been of value to the rest, the day of youth and seeking was gone and the rest felt a certain security in their very lack of creedal faith. They were out in a world of love of neighbor and they wanted to stay there. Being generous-hearted people, they could not bear to believe any longer that man is born totally de-praved, that his nature is essentially corrupt, and all his actions, springing from the devil, are nothing but evil. Their tragedy, and the tragedy of all whom they so profoundly influenced, is that the humanitarianism they thought so satisfying proved to be merely human, and their worship of God grew less and less important to them as love of man became more and more important.

Thus the writers who ignore the religious basis of this era have never quite got at the truth, despite the results of their monumental research and their erudition. It is as if they showed us an assortment of beautiful beads, but with no chain to link them, to give them design or even a decorative usefulness.

An historian writing of that day would mention the mobs and the "No Popery" excitement, although these movements were often political and engineered by selfish men or bigots to stir up the masses. There would be no reason for him to mention the interior confusion of the intellectuals. Again, a writer on sociology might refer to the crowds of penniless and ignorant Irish immigrants who swept into New England, without speaking of religion. But when a man writes of the Concord School, why it was, what it was, and completely ignores the element of religion, he himself lacks "a focus, a moral." He has not explained why men reared in Calvinism, a faith based on belief in the supernatural, became in one short generation Unitarians or Universalists or Transcendentalists or Free Thinkers or Humanists — or Catholics. One can understand George Shuster's remark : "The Calvinist Jonathan Edwards, who believed in the Devil, bequeathed Tradition to Emerson, who believed in man !"

That is the trouble with books like Mr. Brooks' : they

seem to deal with facts and history, and actually give a
mass of fascinating incidents ; yet they make no mention
of the basic reason why people acted as they did.   They
make, as Mr. Commager observes, "impressionism subli-
mate to scholarship."   It is easy to tell the story of a mob
and why it has been worked up to become a mob.   It is
a different thing when the mob is, so to speak, a mob of
thoughts in a man's mind.   It is not so easy to say who
put them there and how he let them get there, and it does
seem unfair and careless to write as if, to quote Mr. Shuster
again, "tradition was tossed like some carefully wrapped
parcel from the Puritan Mayflower."

    For instance, in Mr. Brooks' books there is only passing
word about Isaac Hecker.   Yet Emerson thought him of
enough importance to work hard to keep him from the
Catholic Church, talked to him, went to see him at Mrs.
Thoreau's where he was boarding, took him on a jaunt to
the Shaker settlement, asked him biting questions about
the Faith.   In Henry Seidel Canby's life of Thoreau there
is no mention at all of Hecker.   Yet, under Hecker's
pleading, Thoreau no doubt at one time came quite close
to Catholicism, almost yielding to the idea of a trip to
Rome to study the old monuments of that Faith.   Years
later Hecker said of him that under Catholicism he would
have been a minor St. Francis, but as it was he never
learned to distinguish between nature and nature's God.
No one ever quotes that, nor does Mr. Canby or Mr.
Brooks cite from the excellent and shrewdly worded material on transcendentalism in Hecker's later writings.

Yet Hecker was a transcendentalist ; his viewpoint should have been at least worthy of mention by men who consider themselves historians of a period.

When Frothingham's *Transcendentalism in New England* was published in 1876, Hecker poked gentle fun at the author for writing a whole book and never once having understood his subject. The author traced transcendental teaching to Kant and Cousin and Coleridge and Carlyle. Hecker says it was indigenously American and in New England it was only the "righteous and earnest protest of our native reason in convalescence against a false Christianity on account of its absurd dogmas and its denial of rational truths."

Hecker thought that many New Englanders had deserted the denominations in which they were born due to considerations particularly American, since our American institutions emphasize the assertion of man's natural rights, his noble gift of liberty and his intrinsic worth. Eventually this American idea won against the imported Calvinistic beliefs with their distrust of human nature. The only trouble was that at the same time was lost their belief in the supernatural ; and in order to fill that void with something more than merely love of neighbor they took up odd cults and 'isms. Channing felt that herein lay the failure of the transcendentalists, at the very time they should have become an important factor in American life. In identifying themselves with foreign doctrines, the life of an original movement was lost.

They had been taught that Calvinism was the true and

genuine interpretation of Christianity. If one denied total depravity and election one had to deny the whole thing. The divinity of Christ was among such doctrines, so these New Englanders felt they had also to deny the divinity of Christ.

Why did they not turn instead to the Catholic Church? Why did they do so in only isolated instances? They were scholars, many of them. They knew Latin and Greek and could have read the early Fathers and St. Thomas. In his book, written in 1876, Mr. Frothingham says that "Romanism had no hold on the thinking people of Boston. None besides the Irish laboring and menial classes were Catholics, and their religion was regarded as the lowest form of ceremonial superstition." Frothingham characterizes the Unitarians of New England as "good scholars, accomplished men of letters, humane in sentiment and sincere and moral in intention." A number of the persons whose biographies follow in this book certainly come within that category so far as intelligence and moral intention and breeding are concerned. Yet they were New Englanders too, and Frothingham mentions none of the prominent Catholics of his day.

What such writers as Octavius Frothingham and Van Wyck Brooks could not and cannot see is that even the smallest and poorest Catholic church represents one great fact — the continuity of the Christian Faith. In one way or another, each of the converts mentioned here was attracted to the Catholic Church by the consideration of its continuity. Sarah Peter found that continuity when she

saw the catacombs ; Sophia Ripley found it when she read
Dante.  Some of the Episcopalians, attracted by the
ritual of their denomination, remained where they were
so long as they believed it had continuity.  When their
eyes were opened, they no longer dallied there.  Others
found evidence of the Catholic Church's continuity in
various places, but this one great fact had to come home
to them first, no matter what the argument or what beauty
or pain or joy first drew them.  The altar light gleaming in a shadowy church is but a symbol pointing to a
Faith, not the Faith itself.

There are many other important American converts to
Catholicism not mentioned in this book.  The list of converts among the officers of our Army and Navy alone, in
all the years since the Revolution, is amazingly long.  But
the people written about here fall into the group affected
in one way or another by the American tradition of culture and of democracy.  In a time when Catholicism was
looked on as a foreign sect, they saw what it really was :
the universal Church of mankind, not of Italy but of the
world.

# CONTENTS

# IN NO STRANGE LAND

# LEVI SILLIMAN IVES
## [1797–1876]

*"The necessary abiding unity."*

Since his consecration in 1831 at the age of thirty-four as the first Bishop of North Carolina, Levi Silliman Ives had been a leading figure among the Protestant Episcopal clergy. In 1852 at the age of fifty-five, he was received into the Catholic Church, the first Protestant bishop since the Reformation to became a Catholic. With his wife he went to Rome to make his submission to Pope Pius IX, thus abandoning, as he himself said, "a position in which he had acted as a minister of the Protestant Episcopal Church for more than thirty years, and as a bishop of the same for more than twenty, and sought late in life admission as a layman into the Holy Catholic Church, with no prospect before him, but simply peace of conscience and the salvation of his soul."

Levi Ives was born in 1797, the eldest of ten children of a well-to-do farmer whose English forebears had settled in Massachusetts in 1648. As a boy he went to the academy near his home in Meriden, Connecticut, and although still very young he enlisted in the War of 1812 toward the end of that conflict. After serving in the army for a year, he entered Hamilton College with the intention of becoming a Presbyterian minister.

However, during the next few years he grew greatly dissatisfied with the Presbyterian forms of belief, and

became more and more filled with an idea being widely
discussed at that time, namely, that Protestantism would
never become a dominant part of Christianity unless it
took on again some of the doctrines discarded at the time
of the Reformation.   On the other hand, the Roman
Catholic Church had taken on so many errors during the
centuries — so ran the argument — that it was disqualified as an acceptable faith.   The Protestant Church had
cast away too much, but it could easily add those doctrines which it felt necessary to salvation, and so regain
the importance of early Christianity.

The result of Levi Ives' study of various sects was that
he became an Episcopalian, since that church seemed
to be nearer his ideal of a combination of the new and
the ancient faiths, the one which held in it the best of
the old Catholicism and of the newer Protestant beliefs.
He decided to become a minister, and Bishop Hobart of
New York interested himself in the young man.   Ives
completed his religious studies at the old Chelsea Seminary in New York, was ordained in 1823, and after one
brief year at a small church, was named rector of Christ
Church in Philadelphia.   A year before he had married
Rebecca Hobart, the Bishop's daughter and a godchild
of Mrs. Elizabeth Seton, whom Dr. Hobart had so strenu-
ously tried some years before to prevent from entering
the Catholic Church.   In 1831 Dr. Ives became the first
Episcopal Bishop of North Carolina.

From the start Bishop Ives' deepest interest was in education.   Wherever he could he opened schools for boys

and for girls too.   He also took a deep interest in the wel-
fare of the slaves, and saw that they had as much religious
training as he could bring them.   And wherever he spoke
or taught he always tried to model his teachings on those
of the early Christian church.

At this time in Wisconsin, at Nashotah, a ritualistic
group in the Episcopal Church had succeeded in setting
up a religious community which observed a sort of monastic life that was both ascetic and missionary in scope.
Having watched this experiment with deep interest,
Bishop Ives decided to attempt the foundation of the
same sort of community in his own diocese.   He called
the little community he began at Valle Crucis, the Brotherhood of the Holy Cross.   In 1845 he outlined very carefully to the diocesan convention what his institution was
setting out to do : it was to give simple instruction to
poor children ; to recruit from the diocese men of talent
who could later act as teachers and catechists, and also to
train boys for the ministry.   He hoped for a model farm
as a help to the surrounding communities, and perhaps
later for an agricultural school.

Before five years had gone by, opposition to his plan
was loud in the Episcopal communion in the south and
east.   Roman Catholic practices were reported to be increasing at Valle Crucis and it was the Bishop himself,
ran the complaint, who was sanctioning them.   A senator from Connecticut wrote a bitter pamphlet about it —
"a black cassock extending from throat to ankles, akin
to that of the Romish order of Jesus ; a pyx on the altar

where are reserved the remaining consecrated elements ;
a celibacy of the young men insisted on ; manuals of devotion with prayers to the Virgin Mary." Worst of all,
it was rumored that a curate in the diocese had written a
prayer to the Virgin Mary, no doubt fired by the example
of his bishop. From Valle Crucis, Bishop Ives sent forth
a pastoral letter, not an actual answer to these charges,
but no doubt so intended. In the letter he upheld the
doctrine of the Real Presence, of prayers for the dead and
other practices, and he spoke affectionately of the Episcopal liturgy, "fairly interpreted by the creeds and the Coun-
cils of the primitive church."

Then the storm became a hurricane. The Bishop
continued to protest his loyalty to the Episcopal Church
and kept up his endeavors to show his doubting brethren
that everything he taught and told them was only a part
of the early church of which the Episcopal Church was
the successor. But unfortunately for his own peace of
mind, the more he sought for better arguments to convince them, the more uneasy he himself became. Eventually, in 1852, he told the diocese that he must have a
leave of absence for six months : his health was impaired
and he was in need of a rest. His friends hoped he would
come back cured. His enemies said there was little hope
for a cure from Roman fever for a man so far gone with
the disease as Bishop Ives.

During the next months he wrote a short book which
he called *The Trials of a Mind in its Progress Towards*

*Catholicism.* In it he spoke over and over again of the one thing that moved him most to leave his own loved communion, the fact that Our Lord had so deep a love and compassion for the poor — "Go to the poor," He had said — and that the Protestant church was doing very little in the way of charity. He felt the "utter incompatibility of the system in which I act compared with Christ's mission to the poor." His own efforts to aid the poor in his diocese had been misunderstood by his fellow clerics.

With all his heart he had hoped to stay where he was, but he saw how impossible that had become. "When I ask for authority I find only individual opinion — for unity, division, and mutual recrimination — no agreement even in narrowest sectarianism."

Once, while he was trying to make up his mind whether to go or stay, he heard of a threat that angered him : he was a poor man, rumor said, so perhaps he could be brought to terms by starvation. "Mrs. Ives and I — thank God she stands by me — will submit to any hardship. However tightly you fasten the screws on me, you will not find me guilty of simony," he lashed at the mean-minded.

His reading had for years been from Protestant sources but during his last years as Bishop he had begun to read Catholic works to learn more of the primitive Church. And he had of course been for some years a reader of works of the leaders of the Oxford Movement and knew many of its exponents in the United States. The seminary from which he had graduated had its quota of New-man men.

But now, the more he tried to read Catholic works the more uneasy he became about his own position, and he prayed that God would soon lead him to a place of safety, for he saw he was standing on very uncertain ground. He saw in his sect disagreement not on superficial things but only on fundamentals.

He saw that no mere approximation of the truth would help him to stay. And finally he wrote wearily, "I had had enough. My mind reached forth for a distinct and infallible response ; and it did so confidently and with a sense of right, for under God's invitation and promise it reached forth to God and to God alone." He had found the "necessary abiding unity."

When his decision was reached he announced that he was severing his connections with the Episcopal Church and accepted the invitation of Pius the Ninth to come to Rome to be received into the Catholic Church. Before he went, in December of 1852, he left a letter which was to serve as a record of his conversion in case he died on the way to Italy. With him went his wife, whose well-being was one consideration which had delayed him so long on his way to the Church. Naturally the Hobarts bitterly fought his move. But though Mrs. Ives herself felt very little interest in Catholicism, she had a deep love for her husband, and where he went there she, who was a bishop's daughter and had been a bishop's wife, went too.

There is still to be found a pamphlet containing a sermon preached at Pottsville, Pennsylvania, to the congregation of Trinity Church at the ceremony of deposition of Bishop Ives. It is entitled : "A Man of God was disobedient unto the Name of the Lord." It is very long and full of paragraphs about King Jereboam and those who in his day did not listen to "princely invitations to idolatry." It quotes the Apocalypse : "the mystery, Babylon the great."

No doubt what most annoyed the Episcopal bishops was that Bishop Ives had dedicated his own little book to them — "to my late brethren and to all who pray to be led into the way of truth." "I have loved you well," he wrote, "I have labored for you earnestly. Now I pray He may ere long make you partakers of the new and unutterable joy I now feel when I declare that I believe in the Holy Catholic and Apostolic Church."

The May following his departure for Rome and his reception into the Catholic Church, Dr. Kirby of the Irish College wrote to Bishop Fitzpatrick of Boston that Dr. Ives was still there and was well and firm in his faith ; that Mrs. Ives was still in her old belief but much changed for the better. Dr. Kirby said she was quite happy now to meet priests and hear them even on religious subjects, and was sure she would be a Catholic now were her American friends not so busy writing her anti-Catholic letters.

One thing bothered Dr. Ives very much. He knew he must return home soon, and he would come back a very poor man, his high rank gone, and with a wife to support on practically no income. And he was almost sixty years old.   The same question also caused concern to the Catholic Bishops of the United States who were trying to get together from their own meager incomes a sort of subsistence for Dr. Ives.   That good plan fell through, chiefly because the Bishops were all so poor themselves.   Archbishop Hughes did the practical thing : he procured for Dr. Ives two part-time teaching positions, one at St. Joseph's Seminary, the other at the Academy of Mount Saint Vincent.

Thankful though he was for these efforts, Dr. Ives was working out his own future.   He wanted to devote a part of his time at least to the aid of the poor, and he hoped he could especially help children, for the education of children he had always considered as his life work.   First of all, in order to affiliate himself with some organization whose work was along the line he intended to follow, he joined the Society of Saint Vincent de Paul.

With his whole heart he took up a problem then agitating the Society : the condition of immigrant children. The immigrants from many lands needed pastors and churches and instruction for their children, and New York felt these needs the most keenly of all the dioceses.   Archbishop Hughes was doing his best, but the need was greater than his best, for the immigrants were coming in such waves that the Church could not have built fast enough even had it the money, which it often had not.   So the public school and the Protestant mission often took the Catholic child in charge.

Archbishop Hughes had great need of missionaries and

Sisters ; he never had nearly enough. But now at least he had a layman of experience and deep faith to aid him. And the Vincentians too found Dr. Ives a great inspiration. They had been organized in the New York diocese less than ten years before, and each year they had grown more appalled at the conditions the members met each day as they tried to alleviate only a little the conditions — crowding, misery, and hunger — of these poor. In a short time Dr. Ives put into practice a practical method of coping with the problem, using to help him the background of his years of experience among the poor in the South. He set out to interest important laymen in the work of keeping and reclaiming the Church's neglected small ones. The diocese gave him all the help it could, as well as three hundred dollars a year for the expenses of his work. Finally he saw the founding of a Society — the Society for the Protection of Destitute Catholic Children in New York — an organization that was to be in charge of twenty-six lay trustees and a chaplain. It took more hard work to get the charter from the legislature, but it was secured, and in the spring of 1863 the board of trustees elected Dr. Ives their first president. The next year the institution received for the care of children fifteen thousand dollars from the city and a smaller amount from the state.

Dr. Ives had found the niche where he could be of most value to the Church. He proved an excellent speaker and popular among Catholics, both laity and clergy. They were attracted by his humility, and there was spiritual romance in his coming from the dignity of a bishop to that of a simple layman. Before long his idea of a Catholic Protectory for children was taken up by other cities. Those who had money were willing to trust it to him to disburse, to carry out his ideas. Those who had none trusted him too, for he went down among them and worked with them. He took literally still his Lord's command — "go to the poor."

That the Catholic child must have a Catholic education was the main plea of his every speech, his every endeavor. The child's religion must come first in his life. And Dr. Ives had a right to speak thus, for he knew how great a thing it was to hold the truth and how even greater it must be never to lose it at all.

"Plato and Aristotle taught us," he said in an address at Cooper Institute, "as pure a morality as is professedly taught by that neutral system in our common schools. Why is the teaching of Our Blessed Lord better? I will tell you. He not only teaches the right way, but also prescribes means to enable us to walk in it. The philosophy of paganism may have supplied good thoughts, but that of Jesus Christ provides, in addition, the power of good action."

For most of their later years the Ives lived in St. Joseph's Cottage on 138th Street, where the house became a favorite meeting place for converts, and where the first Converts' League was planned. Everyone with an interest in Catholic Charities came here to discuss problems and theories, and from other cities came leaders to talk their problems over with Dr. Ives.

When he died in the autumn of 1867, his funeral was attended by the Archbishop of New York, and bishops from many other dioceses. Archbishop McCloskey, speaking after the Mass, emphasized again how Dr. Ives had loved the poor — "he felt with a deep earnestness the words of the Master — 'the poor you have always with you.'"

After lying in state at the Cathedral, he was buried on the grounds of the Catholic Protectory in Westchester. It was fitting that he should lie here, for he had been its founder, and he had never failed in his devotion to the poor and neglected children of New York.

# SARAH WORTHINGTON KING PETER
## [1800–1877]

*"My conversion is only a return to old ways."*

Sarah Anne Worthington was born in a small cabin in Chillicothe, Ohio, in the spring of 1800. Her father and mother had come to this small village of the Northwest Territory because they had freed their slaves and not wanting to see them set adrift, had brought them as free men to a part of the country which especially forbade slave holding. The birth of Sarah Anne took place shortly after her parents reached the Ohio wilderness and before there was time to build the large mansion which her father, Major Thomas Worthington, was planning. Others of the family came with them or followed later, bringing plate, china, and costly furniture. On the land that the Major bought he began to build a palatial estate, which his wife called 'Adena,' the Persian name for Paradise.

A few years after the Worthingtons came to Ohio Territory, Sally Anne's father was elected to the Assembly in Cincinnati, which necessitated frequent separations from his wife, who was left alone to look after the growing family. When Sally Anne was seven his term was over and he came home again to stay, and devoted much time to enlarging and landscaping his beautiful estate.

The Worthingtons had many visitors from the South

and the East. The Henry Clays of Kentucky came every year ; Dolly Madison's sister was a frequent visitor, and so was the sister of Mrs. John Quincy Adams. Once the Indian chief Tecumseh and his fellow braves came, but insisted on spending the night on the lawn.

For a time Sally Anne and her sister were sent to a boarding school in Kentucky, the headmistress of which was Mrs. Louise Keats, a relative of the poet. Mrs. Keats was a great lover of the Church of England and imparted to her students a knowledge of and admiration for its ritualistic practices and liturgy then being revived by the Oxford Movement. The Worthingtons themselves were devout Protestants and members of the Methodist church at Chillicothe, the only church there. Bishop Asbury often stayed at Adena while on his preaching trips.

When Ohio was made the seventeenth State of the Union, Thomas Worthington was chosen its first United States Senator. His prolonged absence in Washington was so painful to his family that when he was re-elected in 1811, he took them with him to Washington to live. Sally Anne, one day in 1812, sat in the Senate gallery and heard her father protest against an immediate declaration of war against England. In 1814 he was elected governor of Ohio, with Chillicothe as his temporary capital.

Sarah Anne Worthington was married when she was just past sixteen to Edward King, the twenty-one-year-old son of Rufus King, who had been a member of the Continental Congress and later appointed first minister to the Court of St. James. Her father gave them a house on the Adena estate and Edward, admitted to the bar, set about to practise his profession. Two sons were born to them and then a daughter, Mary, who lived to be less than two years old. The death of this child was a bitter blow, for though several brothers followed her, no more girls came to bless the union.

Edward was a devout Episcopalian and Sarah joined that religious fellowship, working hard to prepare the church for Communion service and making altar linens. At twenty-five she was a handsome, poised woman who frequently entertained distinguished guests in her home. Many of these were national figures, for her husband had entered the political scene, and in 1830 he was elected to the Ohio Senate.

For a short time the family spent much time in Columbus, then a thriving village of some twenty-five hundred inhabitants. They sent Rufus and Thomas to the Kenyon Academy at Gambier. Sarah liked the church atmosphere of the college there, whose founders were just establishing a seminary for the Episcopal Church. Sarah at first enjoyed the simple services, but still retaining the love of ritual her headmistress had given her when she was a little girl, she was growing more and more interested in the High Church movement which Bishop Chase of Ohio was fostering.

In 1861 the Kings moved to Cincinnati, making that their winter home. It was a fairly large city and an active one, a town which charmed even the hard-to-please Charles Dickens when he visited what its admirers called the "Queen City of the West." Their summers were still spent back at their loved Adena, but gradually Cincinnati began to seem like home to them. The one thing Sarah regretted was that Bishop Chase had had to resign because of differences with his very Low Church faculty at Kenyon, where her boys were still studying.

The Kings became a part of the pleasant group of men and women who held what was called the Semicolon Reunions — they met to discuss world events, politics, and religion, with sponge cake, coffee, and Madeira as the simple refreshments. However, such diversions and the management of her home did not occupy all of Sarah's time. She had been trained by her mother in a life of Christian service, so she interested herself in a Protestant orphan asylum where she went almost daily to help care for the little ones and take them gifts ; and she was made superintendent of the Episcopal Sunday School in the city.

In 1836, the same year that her son, Rufus, was ready to enter Harvard, Edward King died at the early age of forty. He was buried in the family cemetery at Adena and his grief-stricken widow rented her house in Cincinnati and moved to Cambridge where her second son was also preparing for Harvard.

Sarah King spent pleasant years in Cambridge but she always felt herself an alien. "I am in a Yankee desert," she wrote to her mother. "Do not laugh at my strange expression, but the New Englanders are so queer and peculiar that I feel I should weep for joy to see an old friend." Even the church she loved seemed alien. "The church is in a low state. The whole region is I fear Unitarian. The clergy are either sceptics or they fear to proclaim the fundamental principles of the gospel. Instead they preach morality and earthly motives for the correction of vice. My own blessed church is in sackcloth and ashes and infidelity has full sway. I daily pray for a grace to preserve my faith inviolate."

In the spring of 1837 she bought a home in Cambridge with a wide verandah and a spacious lawn sloping down to the Charles River. Her two boys were with her and so was her youngest brother, Francis, also a student at Harvard. Sarah enjoyed the youthful life in the house, but she cared little for a general social existence. However, she sometimes went into Miss Elizabeth Peabody's Foreign Bookshop for a talk with that clever woman. She read French and German with Mr. Longfellow who liked her very much and said she was "a very attractive woman with an intellectual style of beauty which leads one quite captive." She had long talks with Washington Allston, the painter, who was the only man in irreligious Cambridge with whom she could discuss spiritual matters, for he was an old-fashioned and devout Episcopalian.

In 1840 Mrs. King and her family left Cambridge and she spent some time visiting her mother. She then took a trip to Havana and returned to Philadelphia, where she met William Peter, the British consul there, who was a widower with grown children in England. In 1844 she married him from her old home at Adena.

Now in Philadelphia her social life was filled, and she

spent the summers resting at Newport. But gradually the Peters withdrew from social functions when they could, preferring to enjoy together their literary tastes in evening reading and in working on the English compilation of the classic poets which Mr. Peter was arranging. During the day she managed to do some social work, being especially interested in the Rosine Home, supported by Quakers for unfortunate women. She aided too in establishing the Philadelphia School for Design so that women might have additional professions open to them, and this institution led the movement that resulted in the establishment of schools of industrial art for women throughout the country. At first this experiment was conducted in her own home but later she collected funds to provide a building for the school, and was aided in this work by Mrs. Hale, the editor of *Godey's Lady's Book*. Mrs. Peter was happy to have her as an active and sympathetic co-worker, for from some women she met with no help but almost with hostility. "They do not stand by their sex," she said in deep annoyance.

In 1851 her son Thomas died at the age of thirty and his death was a crushing blow to Sarah Peter. To assuage her grief her husband took her to Europe. It was her first trip abroad. She loved the cathedrals and the green country of England and she would have liked the great estates too had she not seen behind them the bitter poverty of the workers. "No negro in the slave states would condescend to live in such wretched hovels," she wrote. In Belgium and at Heidelberg she was delighted to find her French and German good enough to be understood by the natives.

After a brief stay in London, she decided to travel further, her husband preferring to wait in England until she returned. She decided on a trip to Italy and roamed happily through that country. In Rome the American colony made her very welcome — the Crawfords, the James Lowells, Hiram Powers, William Story. But in January she chronicled "an anniversary of buried hope" in her diary — the date of the death of her daughter Mary.

Once on a drive with friends she met Pope Pius IX, taking a constitutional, garbed in a long robe of white wool and a scarlet hat and scarlet shoes. Their carriage stopped and they rose and bowed, and he smiled and raised his hand in blessing. Mrs. Peter liked the appearance of "his really benevolent face." Later an audience was arranged with the Pope, and His Holiness told her he had heard of her works of charity, and blessed her for them and spoke of the Catholic Bishop of Cincinnati, Purcell.

She returned to England, but only to begin travelling again, this time to Egypt and down the Nile, which she found "as nearly as possible another Mississippi, with palm trees instead of cottonwoods." She reached Jerusalem in time for the Holy Week ceremonies : here she went to all the holy places and paid a visit to the Patriarch of Jerusalem. Then she and her husband went back to the United States, but after a few months in Philadelphia Mr. Peter was suddenly taken ill and died in 1853.

After this bereavement Sarah dismantled her home and returned to Cincinnati. Little by little she entered again into the life of the city, and her house became a salon for those who enjoyed art, letters, and good conversation. When the city planned an art gallery and several citizens made liberal donations to buy works of art for it, Mrs. Peter offered to go at her own expense to Europe and select pictures and casts. From Paris she went to Rome and on a steamer met a number of ecclesiastics on their way to Rome, among them the Redemptorist, John Neumann, later Bishop of Philadelphia. Shipboard conversations with him first turned her mind seriously toward the Catholic Church. She had been troubled in spirit ever since her trip through Palestine and, even before she left Philadelphia after Mr. Peter's death, she had called on Bishop Purcell to talk with him regarding her spiritual life. He suggested she might receive some instruction in the Faith, but thought she should first seek advice from some of the Bishops she would meet in Rome. He also gave her a letter to Archbishop Hughes of New York.

In Rome, after she had selected casts and pictures for the gallery, she called on the Bishops and thought Neumann and Hughes were both "dear good old men." She met Monsignor Bedini, to whom she had letters, and also Cardinal Barnabo. She spent hours on Ash Wednesday on her knees at Saint Peter's, considering her spiritual course, trying to make up her mind.

The thing that finally brought Mrs. Peter into the

Catholic Church was a visit to the catacombs. There she saw in concreteness and reality the continuity of worship and dogma of the Christian Church. When she told Archbishop Hughes of her intention, he arranged a retreat for her at the Convent of the Trinità dei Monti.

She wrote reassuringly to her son of her change of faith, telling him that he knew she was steady and considered in other things and was in this too. "Now as I come nearer to the clear light of truth I marvel that I should always have been so near and yet never discovered it." But it was for her really only "a return to old ways," she insisted.

She was received into the Catholic Church on March 25, 1855, and her godmother was Mrs. Archibald Leslie, an English convert. She met many of the converts from that land during these months — the Marchioness of Lothian, Mr. William Palmer who had come to Rome to form a union of Greek and Anglican churches and went home a Roman Catholic, two young priests from Oxford, John Wynne and William Coleridge, who later became Jesuits. But the thing that most interested her in Rome, aside from her own conversion, was the work which the Order of the Good Shepherd was doing for unfortunate women. She told herself that she meant to "spend the rest of my life in doing good work for the poor Magdalens."

Before she left Rome she had an audience with the Pope, as a Catholic now, and he was happy to learn that she meant to devote the rest of her life and her fortune to the promotion of religion in the United States. She went on to Paris and visited the motherhouse of the Good Shepherd order, where she carefully studied the house, the grounds, the methods of administration.

In Cincinnati the Semicolons received her with a wary eye, considering her change of religion, but there were other conversions there since she had gone : the Tractarian movement had found disciples in America, and more than one non-Catholic had followed Newman's lead, in Cincinnati as elsewhere.

Mrs. Peter now went to see Bishop Purcell and told him she wished to help the spiritually destitute, especially the women prisoners in jails, that she wanted to put in practice the good work she had seen accomplished in Europe where in one prison eight hundred women were in the charge of the Sisters.   She petitioned the order in America for help and secured five Sisters for a foundation in Cincinnati.   The Sisters in their white robes at first caused a minor sensation in the city, but before long they went their way unnoticed and the house was running well. The city now sent them women to care for as well as delinquent girls and children from broken homes.

That work in competent hands, the busy convert turned to another field — the care of the sick and suffering poor. She consulted Bishop Purcell about a foundation of the Sisters of Mercy who had done valiant nursing in the Crimea, and went herself to the motherhouse in Dublin to ask for Sisters.   The Mother General was unable to grant her request, but suggested she try one of the other Irish houses.   In Cork she was likewise unsuccessful, but at Kinsale met with more encouragement though no definite promise.

On the eve of sailing for the Continent, she heard in London of a new congregation — the Little Sisters of the Poor, who cared for aged and destitute men and women. She paid their motherhouse in Brittany a hurried visit, resulting in a promise that some of the Sisters would come to Cincinnati as soon as funds were provided for them. Later in Rome she discussed these plans with the Pope and asked his approbation of the project, for the Sisters of the Poor were begging Sisters. She got the permission and a blessing and a goodly sum of money to help establish the foundation. She wrote home, "I fancy he begins to regard me as quite an old acquaintance."

After securing varying sums for her Sisters from royalty and nobility and commoners — for no one was safe from Mrs. Peter who said herself of these trips that she "fished busily" — she visited Austria too and cast her net there; this time an Empress responded. The Royal palace at Dresden was equally generous. In Bavaria King Louis gave her a thousand florins.

Back in Ireland she found she was to have her Sisters of Mercy and they all set sail for New York, whence they entrained for Cincinnati, where Mrs. Peter put up her new Sisters in her own home, as she did every new group until a house was found for them.

She was fifty-eight years old now, but as eager to travel as ever. She decided to visit in her own country seeing friends in the East ; and in Jersey City in the summer of

1858 she met a notable group of New England converts :
George Ripley's wife Sophia ; John McMaster, editor of
the *Freeman's Journal* ; Orestes Brownson, booming and
logical ; and the convert priest, Isaac Hecker, who had just
established his Paulist congregation of missionary priests,
the first religious community for men founded in America.
She enjoyed herself among them and would have stayed
longer but word came of a new group of Sisters arriving in
Cincinnati, the Sisters of St. Francis, and she had to go
home to find a house for them. These Sisters were to
do nursing work, and by hustling and "fishing" Mrs.
Peter succeeded in getting them not only a house but
money for a hospital, the cornerstone of which was laid
in 1859.

As all three communities of her Sisters were now established, Mrs. Peter for a time had her house to herself.
She began to wonder — and wrote of it right away to
Father Hecker — if it might not be a good idea to found
a feminine branch of his congregation.

It was also time, decided Mrs. Peter, to establish in
Cincinnati an order of cloistered nuns for perpetual adora-
tion ; and she felt that she herself would like to finish her
life in such an order — her especial choice being the
Franciscan Clarisses whom she was hoping to bring to
Cincinnati. It was the Mother General herself who dis-
suaded her, feeling that Mrs. Peter might find it difficult
at her age to adapt herself to the rigorous routine of monastic life and its ascetic requirements. So instead she
offered the Sisters her home, asking if she might live there

as a semi-religious. She set to work as soon as this was agreed upon, to renovate the house, reserving two rooms for herself. Already she had her eye on the grounds next to hers for a church and a convent, and she sold her furnishings to make it financially possible to acquire the property. She drove hard bargains with friends too, but when one of them hesitated because the price of a sofa was really exorbitant, Mrs. Peter said, "Martha, every time you look at that sofa imagine you see a humble Franciscan Sister standing behind it and you'll never regret what you paid for it."

When the cornerstone of the convent was laid in 1861, she wrote to her friend Father Hecker, "There are still two more objects I want to see accomplished. I want to have an asylum for foundlings and a refuge for neglected and delinquent boys under the Trappists in Kentucky."

Suddenly came the Civil War, with its problem of neglected children and soldiers' orphans, and Mrs. Peter urged the Sisters to take them in until another place could be found. Abandoned babies were another problem, but this the Sisters could not deal with, so she made arrangements for these foundlings at Covington until the Sisters of St. Vincent de Paul established a home in Cincinnati.

Her Sisters of Charity went to nurse the wounded ; her Sisters of Mercy rented their convent as a military hospital and nursed there ; her Sisters of St. Francis worked in the military hospitals. And she herself equipped a medical ship and sailed on it with some of the Sisters, working at nursing and scrubbing and feeding, and bringing time and again a cargo of wounded men to Cincinnati.  Hardly did they get a moment of sleep before the words "more wounded" brought them to their feet again.  To the young Southern prisoners she was a second mother, so much so that she had to bear the suspicion from some Northern officials of being a spy.

In 1863 she was at last able to persuade the city to place the women of the prisons under her Sisters of Charity. They were given a miserable building for their use, but they set to work to make it over, to clothe the women and find work for them to do — all with donations raised by Mrs. Peter's valiant fishing.

During the next years she answered requests for Sisters in other cities and through her foundations were established in various parts of the East.  In 1865 she saw a children's home opened.  Then, when she went to the mountains to rest for a while, she found the conditions among the mountain dwellers so terrible that she felt she must aid instead of resting.

Between times, in the two rooms of her old home, she had the pleasure of visits from the grandchildren and the one son left her, Rufus, now a noted jurist like his father. So many had died, some in the war, that the ranks of the once large family were quite thinned.

Suddenly she felt she must see Rome once more.  In 1867 she set out.  She found a warm welcome in the Eternal City.  Cardinal Barnabo was there and Father

Hecker, on his way to a Congress at Belgium. And she saw the Holy Father again. "Ah, Madame Peter," he cried when she entered, *"mi piace molto vidervi moltissimo."*

For two years after she returned home she lived quietly, with time to write letters and to read. She even translated a work on Church history from the French, but anonymously — "It is a gift as an act of thanksgiving for the precious gift of the Faith." There were four large volumes of six hundred pages each. It was a really large gift for a woman nearing seventy.

The following year, hearing that her niece had been ordered a change of climate by her doctor, she took her to Europe, although she had herself recently suffered a slight stroke. She arrived in Rome at a really important time — the Council to define papal infallibility was just convening. Many of the old friends were dead now, but Cardinal Barnabo was still there. Father Hecker was there again, representing a Bishop who could not come ; and Pio Nono welcomed her cordially as ever.

She must have been rather weary now and she knew she was, for she wrote home that she expected from now on to be a cheery old lady and nothing more. However, she paid a short visit to Germany before she sailed for home and here she was caught in the beginnings of the Franco-Prussian War. Nevertheless she managed to get a berth on a French ship and sailed for home, where she learned that due to her efforts one more foundation had come to Cincinnati.    The Religious of the Sacred Heart, whose coming was long urged by Mrs. Peter and Archbishop Purcell, were opening a school in the city.

Last of all, the Passionist Fathers after much urging by the same two people came, and the chronicles of the monastery say that "had it not been for Mrs. Sarah Peter they would never have made a foundation in that town." More than one passage in the same chronicles tells of her generous contributions.

After all this it seems almost incredible to write that she made another trip to Rome, with an American pilgrimage to visit the Pope who, since the sacking of Rome by Italian troops, had been a prisoner in his own palace. She wrote that they were all "well and merry as birds about the ship."    She was also, she wrote, acting as treasurer for the benefit concert on the ship.    It was for shipwrecked mariners, a cause dear to her own heart.

She visited Lourdes first and then hurried to Rome.    "I am making my pilgrim prayers as I hope I should," she wrote.    She was then seventy-four.    It was her sixth journey to Rome.    The Holy Father sent for her as soon as he heard she was in the city.    This time the papers mentioned her presence, writing long articles about her, which displeased her and made her wish her zealous friends would be less demonstrative.    At one grand celebration she happened to be placed quite near the throne where the Pope sat with his Cardinals.    When he saw her, he was heard to say audibly to the man next to him, *"Ecco nostra cara Signora Peter."*

After her return home she lived three years more.  As a member of the Third Order of Saint Francis, she observed that rule to its fullest, and, in her own small chapel, she knelt often in prayer.  She found time to work on vestments which she meant to send the Holy Father for his coming Golden Jubilee.

In 1877, as she was leaving the confessional, she slipped and fell, and, though the accident seemed slight, she failed steadily after it.  One evening she said an especially affectionate good-night to her son and his wife who had come to see her at her request.  Finding that she could not sleep, she decided to make a tour of the house and asked two of the Sisters to go with her.  She went slowly through every room, the chapel last of all.  She stood looking long and intently at the flickering sanctuary light, and then she went back to her room.  In the early morning she sent word that she would like the priest to offer the five o'clock Mass for her.  Before it was ended she was dead.

Archbishop Purcell, who preached her funeral sermon, took as his text, "She hath opened her hand to the needy and stretched out her hands to the poor," and he ended, "I do believe that we have lying before us the remains of a saint, and I would rather myself pray to her than for her."

# SOPHIA DANA RIPLEY
## [1803–1860]

*"Nothing belonging to time
will satisfy the soul."*

Sophia Dana Ripley was born in Cambridge in 1803 ; her parents were members of two distinguished New England families : the Danas and the Willards. Her great grandfather had been a signer of the Declaration, one of her grandfathers a member of the Continental Congress and first minister to Russia, the other a president of Harvard. She had received an excellent education in the classics and excelled both in Greek and modern languages ; she had learned her French and Italian on the Continent. Always an advocate of higher education for women, she opened with her mother and sister a school for advanced studies for girls at what is now Radcliffe College.

When she was twenty-four she married George Ripley. It was a marriage highly approved by her family, for his own background was good and he was a minister of the Unitarian faith for whom on his graduation from the Divinity School ("the" meaning Harvard, of course) a congregation had been assembled and a church built. This was his only parish and he stayed with it for fourteen years and left only at his own insistence that he must. "I can pray no more by the job," he said sadly when his congregation begged him to remain.

Sophia sat in the minister's pew when he made his farewell address, his attempt to make his people understand why he was leaving them. "I do not feel I have succeeded in waking a spirit of mental independence in my parish. I have wanted you to see the truth with your eyes and not with mine. It is not the fault of you people but of the creed which I have been preaching here, as I was taught to preach it. The followers of Jesus should be a band of brothers — a family who do not care about the chief seats in the synagogue. I feel the spirit of God no longer in our churches. My sympathies are with the downtrodden and the poor — and our creed cares little about them. That is why I am leaving you today."

The look in his wife's face gave him courage to finish. "It is not that I have lost faith. I have rather added to it. I believe in the omnipotence of kindness, moral integrity, and divine charity."

George Ripley had decided to put his faith to work. With other men who believed in his idea, he had bought a farm where the transcendental philosophy could be given a practical demonstration, a farm where all would work with hands as well as with head, where hoeing and teaching would be of equal dignity, where no one would be called servant because all would be servants. In an era when being a minister meant being a gentleman and being an artisan or ploughman meant being a peasant, this was a great departure.

But the founders of Brook Farm went ahead with their plans, despite the outcry. Ripley was head of the group and beside him always was his wife Sophia, sweeping when he ploughed, scrubbing the kitchen floor when he scrubbed the cow barn, teaching Italian and French where he taught philosophy.

Tall, fair and slim, she moved among the community in a servant's dress of calico. Sometimes she spent ten hours a day in the laundry, over tubs or ironing boards, lending the place, said Charles Dana, "an air of seductive cheerfulness." And, when one of the young Spanish pupils was thought to have leprosy, it was she who for months washed and bound his wounds until he was better.

On her first evening at the Farm a homesick little girl stood at the dining room door, watching everyone file in. She thought some of the men looked like pictures in an English story book that far away in the South her mother used to show her. Suddenly her tears began to fall, for her mother was dead and she was alone in this dreary place. Then a woman in checked black calico came up to her, stooped and kissed her, and Nora put up her arms and kissed back and trotted happily after Mrs. Ripley into the dining room. Years later she said that though she had never seen such a dress on anyone but a colored domestic at home, it had ever since seemed to her like material for princess's robes.

Brook Farm lasted for three years as a community of high ideals and hard work and excellent schooling, a place where Emerson and Margaret Fuller and Theodore Parker

came to lecture, where for a time Hawthorne and Charles
Dana and George Curtis and Theodore Dwight boarded
for varying intervals.    It lasted a few more years as a very
different place — a community devoted to the ideas of a
Frenchman, Charles Fourier, who had a humanitarian
scheme for putting the whole world into molds of At-
tractiveness and Harmony.   The scheme would seem to
have been a bit military, a bit wonderful, a bit foolish,
and possible only, if ever, with a huge group to carry it
out, thousands, where Brook Farm was composed of less
than a hundred.  To have them try out so grandiose a
scheme was, as the doubting Emerson put it, "a revolution
in a patty pan."

Almost from its beginning Mrs. Ripley had doubts con-
cerning the Fourier idea, but she stayed with the project
because her husband, whom she dearly loved, stayed by it.
But by the time Brook Farm broke up, after a disastrous
fire and the realization that the whole scheme was im-
practical, she had become interested in a very different
philosophy.   For one thing, young Isaac Hecker had
spent some time at the Farm.   He came there at the suggestion of his friend Orestes Brownson, who thought it
was a fine place for him while he was making up his mind
where his future lay — and for Isaac that meant a religious future.

He and Mrs. Ripley were often in the kitchen together,
she scrubbing and he baking bread, and they had long discussions.   Isaac was even then veering towards the Catholicism he later embraced, and though he was at the Farm

only a short time, it was enough to give Mrs. Ripley a
fair knowledge of Catholic belief.   Several others gathered in the kitchen to listen and argue, including Sarah
Stearn, Mrs. Ripley's niece, who was also to become a convert.   One disgruntled lady Swedenborgian who boarded
at the Farm said darkly they would soon be hearing rosa-
ries rattling under aprons out in that kitchen.

Two years later, when Isaac was on his way from Concord to New York he stopped off at the Farm to tell his
friends his plans for the future.   "I am going to enter the
Catholic Church," he said, and began explaining his decision.   Ripley listened with interest, but Isaac thought
that Sophia showed even more warmth and earnestness.
It impressed him because her manner was usually very
calm and unexcited.   He wondered at it, and hoped that
she would be a Catholic some day too.

The Farm experiment, done to death by lack of funds,
by growing distrust of Fourierism, and the disastrous fire,
ended ; and the little group went back to the world again.
Ripley had put all he had in the world into the scheme
and now, after using all the remaining funds to pay bills,
there were still some thousands owing.   He undertook
to pay this, first selling his beloved library so famous in
Boston.

The Ripleys went to Brooklyn and took cheap rooms in
Flatbush.   George wrote editorials for *The Tribune* and
his wife taught classes in modern languages to earn the
money for their simple needs and to pay off the Farm
indebtedness.   In 1849 he became a member of *The*

*Tribune* staff and, with improved fortunes, they went to New York to live and to mingle again with the literary groups they had known.

At the Farm Mrs. Ripley had said little about her religious doubts. She had of course long felt that the transcendental cult was materialistic and nothing else, though framed in lovely phrases and lofty sentiments. She saw it answered none of life's riddles about the future of mankind. She felt there must be some solution and when she saw that Hecker, the transcendental dreamer, and Brownson, the dogged seeker, had alike found one in the Catholic Church, she studied its doctrines further. Although many of them fitted with difficulty into her previous philosophy, she did feel certain of one thing, for which so far the transcendentalists had found no answer : man had not been placed on the earth without reason and somewhere there must be a logical reason for his existence.

"George," she said one day, "they have never found anything but arguments and no contentment at all. Yet they are looking for something even if they deny it, for all of us know in our hearts that we must find an enduring peace of some sort and a content that will make the fact of earthly life worth while."

He smiled with that smile of deepest love he always reserved for her, for of one thing, among many things unsure, Sophia Ripley was sure : she was a greatly beloved woman. "You will find it some day," he told her.

"I hope so. Nothing belonging to time will satisfy the soul of man and we deal here only with time."

One day she heard Theodore Parker quote St. Augustine : "O God, Thou has made us for Thyself and our hearts are restless until they rest in thee." Suddenly it came to her that that was what Dante had meant in those beautiful passages she had loved for so long but thought of only as literature, not as the exponent of a living faith. Dante meant that once you had a real belief in God, you would never ignore it again. She remembered one especially cherished phrase : "One who has looked upon the light cannot turn to other objects willingly."

She went back to Dante and reread him. She knew his works well, for she had held at Brook Farm what was probably the first class in the country which read Dante in the original.

She turned to other authors and began studying the early Fathers in the original Greek. One evening she said excitedly to George, "You should really read some of this and see how continuous it is, and how it is all the same now as it was then — as far back as the second century." But he was content merely to listen to her conclusions. She read and read — books primitive, mediaeval, renaissance, modern, until she could say to her husband with conviction, "George, I am fully persuaded. Here is a Church that is immortal. She has withstood the treason of her own children and the pride of her unworthy servants, and her strength comes from the great love given her by the Saints — and the sinners too."

George had watched her with loving interest but with no desire to follow her. "You will be a strenuous Catholic, Sophie, if you ever join them," he told her one day.

"Join them" she did. Isaac Hecker's impressions had turned out to be not unfounded. In 1847, while he was pursuing his studies for the priesthood in Belgium, he received a letter from Mrs. Ripley announcing her conversion to the Church. It was a letter filled with hope and joy, as if her strong nature hitherto confined and restrained had suddenly been unlocked, as if the veil which had enveloped her was suddenly torn away and her character stood out in all its native sincerity and warmth.

After she came into the Church her devotion was not only for the worship of God, but also to works of mercy for man. Each morning after George left their boarding house in University Place she arranged their rooms, and then spent the rest of the day in busy charity — in hospitals at first and later in the prisons, concentrating after a year on one group, bringing what she called hope to the hopeless, the women victims of their own or men's sensuality. She formed a group of women to aid her and a disheartening task it proved, for they received little encouragement in their work from layfolk and even less from some of the clergy. But they kept on working together until a group of religious, the Sisters of the Good Shepherd, an order then almost unknown in New York, came to make a foundation there and offered to take the work under their charge. A house was found for the Sisters on Fourteenth Street and Mrs. Ripley made it her job to collect money for the rent until the group could be self-supporting.

She had chosen Saint Catherine of Genoa as her patron when she came into the Church, and she now found time in her busy life to translate from the Italian this saint's life and writings. When Hecker heard about this, he thought her a fitting person to do this work. "She is like Catherine," he said, "intellectually great, having charity for the abandoned, and using her pen for God." She loved best the saint's *Treatise on Purgatory* — "the utterance of one immersed in the expiation of love," she said of it. When Isaac Hecker came back to the United States, a Redemptorist priest, she smiled at him at their first meeting. "I am without doubt the only convert you and Dante have made between you," she told him.

Through the years that followed he was her confessor, and she was often of great help to him in various ways. Next to George, he was no doubt the person who understood her best, and who saw that under her reserve were the most elevated of sentiments, that her desire to realize a social life more noble than that ordinarily practised in the world was what had led her to take so full a share in the menial duties of the Farm. He used to say in later years that the one thing he always remembered about her was her striking dignity of manner and her strong high purpose in everything.

In 1854 she became very ill and was found to be suffering from cancer. An operation made her better for a time, but by 1860 she was again very ill and it was obvious that this time she would not recover. During her last difficult days her husband had his desk put into her bedroom and there he worked on his editorials, day after day, often night after night. From November of 1861 to the following February he stayed with her thus in her agony, nursing her, bringing her what relief he could, suffering with her.

"Why don't you complain?" he asked her once, almost angrily.

"But I've nothing to complain of, George," she replied. Ripley had never come into the Church himself, but he had the Last Sacraments brought to her when he knew that the end was near, and he saw that the ground was consecrated in the Dana plot in Cambridge where she was buried.

When he came to the church where arrangements had been made to hold the services, he saw that, almost past belief in its strangeness, it was his own old church into which they carried her. Now a Catholic Church, it had become a very different place from the one he remembered. He sat in the same front pew where Sophie used to sit in the old days; where his pulpit had been, stood her casket. He listened to the words in Latin said over her, words of peace and love and faith. He felt comforted — Sophia was dead, but her spirit had not left him.

He must have been personally moved by the faith she held, for when Isaac Hecker, who had been away in Rome at the time of her death, came to visit him at *The Tribune* office, he asked, "Isaac, can you do anything a Catholic priest can do?" Hecker assured him that he could, and

Ripley said, "Then, when my end is near, if I send for you, will you come to me ?"

Hecker assured him he would, and George did send for him some fifteen years later when he lay mortally ill. But the message was delayed, or perhaps purposely not delivered, and when Father Hecker, hearing of it at last, hurried from the Paulist rectory on Fifty-ninth Street to reach Ripley's side in time, the sick man was too delirious to recognize him and died without regaining consciousness.

Nevertheless Ripley *had* sent for Father Hecker after all the years that had intervened between Sophie's death and his own. She had watched over him tenderly all the years they lived together on earth. There was no reason why that love should not have remained close to him still, or why those prayers should not have followed him.

In her own New England there were many converts before Sophia Ripley and there have been many since. But she stands out among them for special qualities. The understanding and sympathy of the days of her humanistic belief had been greatly increased when she became a Catholic and practised love of God as well as love of human kind. Her inner life was lived on a scale of high endeavor, but she never lost sight of the need of practical works of mercy. She showed in her life as a Catholic an extraordinary ability to organize, and nowhere more than in her work among the women in prisons and hospitals. At first this consisted only of her own personal visits.　When she turned her work over to the Sisters of the Good Shepherd she had established a new way of dealing with the care and regeneration of unfortunate women.

Sophia Ripley was primarily an intellectual, and was recognized as such in her native Boston, where recently a public school has been named the "Sophia Ripley School," and where her pioneer work in the higher education of women is well known.

# ORESTES A. BROWNSON
## [1803–1876]

*"No party but mankind."*

Orestes A. Brownson lived almost a century ago, but he remains peculiarly a man of our own day. His language can be easily understood by those of the present who stand up valiantly, as he did, in an audience of doubters and false dreamers. When he lectured at Concord complaint was made that he was gloomy ; but then Concord always preferred its light bordered with sweetness, and though Brownson insisted on the light, he cared little about the sweetness to embellish it. In retrospect, his gloom seems rather as that of a prophet who grieves for the world than that of a man bewailing his own unhappiness. And one feels that although he would have listened attentively to Isaiah, he would have applauded loudly when Jeremiah spoke.

He was born at Stockbridge, Vermont, in 1803. He and his twin sister Daphne were the youngest of six children. On his father's death the boy's mother gave him to neighbors to be reared and for some years he led a lonely life with this elderly couple. "I had no childhood," he said somberly in later years.

He found in his foster home a small library of Congregational theological works and this turned his thoughts to religion. Instead of the usual child's books, the young lad read solemn treatises on heaven and hell, and com-

43

plicated arguments on election and damnation. He was drawn towards the Methodist Church in the town, but before he could join it, his mother gathered her family together again and took them to live in upper New York, where for a brief time Orestes was able to attend an academy.   It was all he ever had of formal schooling, and he soon left that behind him to go to work in a printing shop, for there was no money for further education.

But his main thought was still on religion, and when he was about eighteen he joined the Presbyterian Church. He kept a diary in those days and it was full of expressions of apprehension and perplexed thinking.   His effort to understand the gloomy doctrines of Knox and Calvin left him mentally tangled.   He was told he must believe man to be totally evil, but he was too logical to believe long in total depravity or in predestination.   And his heart was warm, and he knew in that heart that God is good and that man, made in His image, could not be wholly evil.

"When I was twenty," he said in later years, "and a Presbyterian, and I told clergymen that I could not bear the doctrine that foreordained the wicked to sin necessarily so that God might damn them justly, they told me that the only way they could retain their own faith was by refusing even in their own minds to reason on the subject."

He taught school for a few years, and then fell into a long and serious illness, in the course of which he began to study Universalism, where he found an utter refutation of all Calvinistic doctrine — no eternal damnation for anyone, but salvation for all and a firm opposition to all things of Calvin's bitter school. He decided to become a Universalist minister and applied for a letter of fellowship as preacher. He was ordained the next year.

For a time he was happy in the sunny clime of Universalism. It was a creed that denied evil altogether and no doubt he basked in it as an utter relief. For three years he preached in its churches, calling himself Christian as they all did, but denying divine revelation, the divinity of Christ, and all belief in a future judgment. He was happy too in the men who became his friends. The great Channing thought highly of his ability. Emerson praised his clear thinking, even when he resented his outrightness of speech, and George Ripley thought so well of him that he offered to preach his sermon of installation as minister of the Universalist Church at Canton, Massachusetts. While in this town he one day was called to examine a young man from Harvard who wanted to teach in the town school.

"Mr. Thoreau is examined and will do and will board with me," he announced. All the following summer the two read German together and talked late together night after night. Young Thoreau was enthralled by the sharp intellect of the older man. "Those weeks were an era in my life," he wrote back gratefully after he went home, "the morning of a new *Lebenstag*."

Brownson was happy to be with people who approved of his views, and his congregation did that fully, but unfortunately he could not long hold these views. Soon he was again restless because he realized that he had not yet found his spirit's true home. He could not stay long in a religious or social atmosphere that did not fill his lungs with the breath of life.

He began to interest himself in the needs of social reform and joined the Workingman's Party in New York, lending his strength to its struggles. Suddenly, despite sneers, he left it, too. "I am leaving it," he retorted to objections, "that I may remain faithful to the workingman's cause. What good will political amelioration be if social amelioration is neglected? And you will never get that by arraying labor against capital. Many of the men are virtually slaves but this is no way to get them out of their servitude."

He objected when, even in that long past day, he came on those who thought the state should take over many of the functions of the family. "They want the state to raise the children," he stormed, "to have them instructed only in what is material and sensible. I want them taught love, disinterestedness, and sacrifice. These will build a state."

When he heard a lecture on the value of a constitution as bulwark of liberty, he only smiled his gloomy smile. "That our liberty is written on paper will be of little avail unless it is written on the heart. Our only hope is for a full development of our free institutions, in the moral soundness of our people," he wrote in an editorial. "Unless we correct this all absorbing avarice of men, we must one day sigh like Athens and Rome under the whip of the despot."

"Besides," he added, "I feel our Declaration of Independence has a wider meaning than our fathers suspected. Equality never did mean that all are born with the same capacities but that all men have a common nature and belong to one common family and have equal rights."

In his lectures, which were becoming quite frequent, he always emphasized the fact that no one should derive a benefit from another without giving a full equivalent in return. He said one day to George Ripley, who without doubt understood and sympathized with him more than any of the rest of the men he knew, "Sometimes I fear even for the Constitution — it is being perverted. There are some things that the body politic must not do if it is to survive — a line that majorities may not pass."

The cultivated people of Boston, who admired his scholarship when they read his articles in the *Boston Quarterly Review* which he had established in 1838, and later in the *Democratic Review*, took it otherwise when he inveighed against the wealthy — against factory owners who were grinding down the poor, against those people who felt that a liberal education should not be given to all.

He knew what it meant to work for an education, to teach himself languages and philosophy, and he resented the airy way they spoke of an education. He felt no doubt some of the resentment of a self-educated man, for his was mostly one of extensive reading only. "A liberal education seems to be one that fits a man to live without labor," he snorted, "and disgust at labor, or try-

ing to live without doing any seems to account for most
of the crimes against property. Labor seems avoided not
so much because of the actual work but because it has become associated with the menial. And the clergy must
bear down on the selfish rich and show them how wrong
they are to be living so."

"You want the clergy to amuse the people with dreams,"
said one irritated minister.

"Be it so," said Brownson soberly, "even dreams are
sometimes from God. If the soul could not fly from the
actual to the possible would there be any improvement
ever in man?"

Education for all he felt was one answer. A nation
could not call itself free if only a part of its people were
educated — not alone with the head but with the hands
too. He wanted better school buildings. "A small box,
eighteen by twenty feet, at a crotch in the road, with four
tiny windows — is that ample accommodation for thirty
to forty students for four or eight years? How can young
thought grow strong there?"

He disapproved soft methods of education and disliked the opportunist type of books remarking that "so
many books are published on men and measures and almost nothing on principles." He said he was glad that
there had been few children's books in his early days and
that he had never read any. "Let old people read them
and find recreation there, but they are damaging for children. They make their thinking too easy for them. We
are beginning now to dilute literature for grown men and

women too — these novels and romances," he said scornfully, for Brownson took his philosophers straight.

More and more he resented the conditions of the working man. His indignation was great when he learned that in New York City a man could be fined and imprisoned because he would not work for the wages offered him. And he felt sorry for the capitalist too, for with the cut-throat business methods in use the latter had little chance to consider his employees. When people said to him that the laboring classes in America had an opportunity to rise in the social scale if they tried, he shook his head. "The class cannot rise — only individual members here and there — and they then become cut-throat capitalists also."

He used to stand and watch the crowds pour out of a factory at the end of day, and ask himself where the proceeds of their labor were going. So little to them — so much to the men who employed them. He saw clearly that worse was coming rather than better, that competition among manufacturers was growing less but that the growth of large corporations was bringing the workers under the control of corporate bodies and that would bring the capitalists closer together and give them even greater control over wages.

To Robert Owen, the wealthy Englishman who had risen from poverty and who came to America eager to disseminate his communistic idea of setting up an ideal community in this new land, he was interested but wary. "Given proper circumstances, we can all be perfect," argued Owen. But Brownson shook his head, though he listened patiently. "I am afraid it is not as easy as that. You think we can all live in paralellograms. You can't start with such complete virtue as a premise anyway. You have to grow into it. And social states are not built over night according to abstract authority. You have to take society as it is and work from there. You can develop but you can't create."

"What do you call society anyway?" asked Owen.

"The union of all for the protection of each," said Brownson.

He had liked very much the ideas of the Brook Farm Community and had followed its earlier years with sympathy. When he was in New York lecturing on labor, he met young Isaac Hecker who, distraught about his future, consulted him regarding his spiritual turmoil. Brownson had suggested that the young man go to Brook Farm for a while.

Isaac had wanted to stay close to Boston if he could, for Brownson was living there at the time. "Then I would not be far from your influence," he told his friend, "from the influence of your mind. With you so near I should feel safe from the transcendentalist influence too. I like it but I don't really trust it."

But after his stay at the Farm, after a brief time at Alcott's Fruitlands and at the Shaker community at Harvard, Isaac felt no easier in mind. "When I speculate where all this is leading me, sometimes I feel I can smile and hope, and sometimes I can only weep and sigh."

Brownson could understand this, for he too was distraught about his faith. He could understand Isaac when the latter wrote to him, "I have reached a state where I consider myself a Christian." And he understood him when later, after Hecker had looked into the tenets of the Episcopal Church, he began to consider himself a Catholic — "Whether Anglican or Roman I do not know — much depends on the Oxford Movement as to whether there is any real choice for me."

For Brownson himself had read deeply the writings of the Oxford men. He too was close to the Church now; he had outgrown all the various Protestant sects, harsh or kindly, that had held him at various times. He had gone beyond the social philosophy of Cousin and his own dream of building a "church of the future," a universal church that would replace and yet embrace all the warring sects; he was past the belief that social reform could come about without moral reform. He had studied much and sought long, and now, near the end of his seeking, he was seeing the true church of the future — and of the present and the past too — the Catholic Church.

He laughed now at his former confreres in the ministry, and called their work merely "Sunday exercises." When Isaac said that perhaps these men had been called by the Holy Ghost to preach, Brownson flashed back, "Blaspheme not the Holy Ghost by saying such automatons are of His calling."

He had lost all his objections to the papacy. The

only thing that still troubled him was that he could not give up hope for the salvation of his friends outside the Church and yet he could not feel sure of it either. He went to Bishop Fenwick of Boston with his difficulties, and the Bishop suggested that since he knew God was just it might be well to leave his Protestant friends in His hands.

"But there is one other thing — if I could only find some excuse for the Protestant Reformation I am sure I would feel better," and he looked appealingly at the Bishop. But Bishop Fenwick, as he shook hands in farewell, said only, "Come and see me again — and if you do find some excuse for the Reformation don't fail to let me know about it."

Brownson told Hecker about the interview. "And the Bishop said not one unkind word about Protestantism, but neither did I win from him any concessions at all. I liked that. Had he been less uncompromising, I fear I would have distrusted his sincerity."

In two weeks he was back with the Bishop again, asking to be prepared for admission into the Church. In October of 1844 he was received. Many smiled when they heard it, saying he would be somewhere else soon, but Dr. Channing shook his head. "All his changes have been not fluctuating but steps in ethical progress," he declared. And in England Newman, who was later to invite him to teach at the Dublin University, did not smile at the news, but thought it of great importance.

"Well," said one jocose Transcendentalist to Brownson, "what have you brought into the church, Orestes?"

"Nothing but my sins," he said soberly.

To George Ripley he opened his heart, for him he could trust. "It was that suddenly I saw that the Church is the body of which Christ is the spirit. I saw that the Catholic is the only Church."

"But hasn't it failed too?" asked Ripley.

"Not unless we choose to give the lie to its Founder. You must reject Christ too, I am afraid, if you reject His Church. I have tried in every possible way to escape this conclusion but I cannot. And besides I see the Catholic Church has ever been the friend of the humble and the poor and friendless — that should convince even you."

But it did not. Ripley, for all his love of humanity, was still too fearful of creed, too mindful of the harsh Calvinism from which he had just recently departed, to risk entering another religious fellowship. Like Emerson, he would have said, "Let us call Christ brother — but by no supernatural title."

Brownson, having found his lasting spiritual home, went his own way, happy now in his interior life, though the state of the world about him still made him brooding and gloomy — and argumentative. How could he help but feel so when his life on earth was dedicated to the motto, "No party but mankind," and when he saw how far from any ideal was the world about him?

He had spoken on this subject one day at Brook Farm, and at the conclusion of his lecture George Curtis, referring to his motto, had asked him, "Do you think that will ever come about ?"

Brownson sighed. "Perhaps it will at the conclusion of a war, such a war as the world has never witnessed and from which the heart recoils in horror. No, I am sure that for long years my doctrines will be condemned almost unanimously. But they will all come to pass some day."

His life in the Church was not to prove always happy. Unfortunately the prelate most close to him suggested a course of polemics for him to follow as a convert — arguments along theological lines rather than the social lines he understood best. He encountered many difficulties as a result of his deficient self-education in philosophical and theological subjects. But when he spoke on social conditions and their amelioration, he was always on firm ground. For he was one of the first advocates in the American Catholic Church of a movement now supported by all its leaders — Catholic social justice. It is a pity that much of his greatness is lost in the mazes of disputation, and that his books, with their mighty messages still fresh and true, gather dust where lesser men are still read.

He was often unhappy at the annoyance and even hatred that his polemics aroused. Priests who at first welcomed his clear mind grew to resent his tactless assumption of superiority, for he could argue in only one way — by trying to knock down the other man's opinions. For such unhappiness he was repaid by the wealth of his

spiritual life, for he loved the Church with all his heart
and spirit. It was his misfortune that he could champion her only with a war cry when the voice of a dove
would have been of greater avail.

There were some too who said he would have been
a more peaceable man had he drunk less strong coffee or
had he gone to bed at a reasonable time instead of writing until three or four in the morning. But it had been
more than coffee that made him sleepless and difficult.

Like his namesake he had been a man pursued, not by
the Fates, but by a deep need to find his spiritual home
and by a great ache to make the world a better place for
people to live in. The former he found after years of
bitter search ; the latter he despaired of winning after
wearying efforts to show men that not wealth but character, not desire for gain but love for the poor and the
defeated, was the criterion for a man.

In his later years, as in his earlier, he wrote much and
brilliantly. He worked with Hecker and Hewit on
their new magazine, *The Catholic World,* and many
of its most brilliant articles were from his pen. He
loved to write — he had always loved it, from his first days
on the *Universalist Gospel Advocate and Impartial In-
vestigator.*

He outlived by some years his wife, the slim dark-eyed
Sally Healy whom he had met while still a Universalist
minister, and who had followed him into the Church.
In later years his children and he were sometimes at
odds, for he became a difficult old man. To the last

his confreres were annoyed at his attacks, and in Boston they were prone to speak disparagingly of him, but they all remembered him with a certain respect, whether for his intellect or his heart or his striking appearance — the tall man, well over six feet, with straight black hair brushed back from a massive forehead, and gray eyes that turned black when he was excited. He wore all his life the same garb — a swallow-tail coat, loose black trousers, an immaculate white handkerchief folded in front, crossed at the back of his neck, and brought around and tied in the front.

He was a hard man to forget, and those who agreed with him and those who did not always remembered him. Isaac Hecker, who had difficulty with the old man in his later days, when he objected to any changing or shortening of his articles for *The Catholic World*, wrote to Henry Brownson, when he heard of his old friend's death, "I owe perhaps more to your father than to any other man in my early life. My friendship and sense of gratitude to him has never been affected by any event during forty years. His love for Holy Church was supreme and his faith was never dim. His record will be great in the sight of God."

# CORNELIA PEACOCK CONNOLLY
## [1809–1879]

*"Let us love one another
and pray."*

Cornelia Augusta Peacock was born in 1809, the youngest among six children of a wealthy Philadelphia banker. Her childhood was happy even though her father and mother both died before she was fourteen years old, for she grew to womanhood in the house of an elder sister who loved her dearly. At twenty-one she was a very pretty girl, with great dark eyes and long brown curls. She fell in love with Pierce Connolly, a young Episcopalian clergyman, and married him despite her sister's disapproval. As a matter of fact the young husband was really a good match, for he was well educated, had a fair income, and a most engaging personality.

His first charge was in Mississippi, where two children, Mercer and Adeline, were born to them. Cornelia and Pierce were a very happy young couple, and very much a part of the social life of the little town of Natchez.

One day Pierce heard from a colleague a very bitter attack on the Catholic faith, and he began to read all he could to form his own judgment, much to the annoyance of his wife who said she thought "all Catholic priests were instruments of the devil, if not the devil himself." But as the months passed, Pierce, poring over church history and theology, began to have greater and greater doubts of the validity of what he was preaching, and little by little Cornelia began to share his views.

Four years after their marriage he resigned his parish and prepared to enter the Catholic Church. His bishop tried to dissuade him, his parishioners, who were devoted to him, tried to hold him, his family and Cornelia's did their best to turn him from this mad intention. But in the end Cornelia was herself so persuaded of the necessity of the Faith in her life that she was unwilling to wait, as Pierce wished to do, and be received during a trip they planned to take to Rome. Instead she was received in the Cathedral at New Orleans, and soon after the Connolly family sailed for Europe, where Pierce was to prepare for his reception into the Catholic Church.

They had excellent letters of introduction and found themselves not only in Catholic surroundings but in the midst of the best of Roman society. Among the people they met were the Earl of Shrewsbury and his family, and the former stood sponsor for Pierce when he was received into the Church and later for both the Connollys at their Confirmation.

From one great church, from one art gallery to the other, the Connollys went rapturously ; together they had an audience with the Pope, Gregory the Sixteenth. Cornelia's profile was the admiration of many artists who sought her eagerly as a subject. Meantime Lord Shrewsbury invited Pierce to go to England with him for a few months, while Cornelia and the children remained in Rome. Mercer was four now, and old enough to visit some of the churches with his mother, and to say his prayers before some of the shrines that had an image of the Infant Jesus.

When Pierce came back from England they decided to travel on the Continent before they went back home. Through Italy and Switzerland they made their way leisurely and in Vienna, June 1837, their second son was born and named John. Almost with his coming bad news reached them from America : because of losses in his family fortunes Pierce's income was suddenly cut to almost nothing and he had to return home at once. He was now greatly disquieted about his future, for he had no profession to fall back on. Cornelia, however, had some income left. She refused to be too much alarmed, and was filled with delight because she was soon to be back in her own home and her own land.

The next six months were difficult, and then Father Point, rector of the Jesuit College of St. Charles at Grand Coteau, offered Pierce the professorship of English at that school. The offer was accepted with joy and the Connollys settled down in a little cottage on the campus. Cornelia learned that the Sisters of the Sacred Heart would be happy to have her instruct their pupils at a nearby school in singing and piano. This, with the small income left to each of them, and with Pierce's salary, provided a sufficient living, and the small family was very happy. In July of the following year a daughter was born and named Mary. To the sorrow of her parents she lived for only a few weeks.

As the months went by Cornelia Connolly became an earnest Catholic, absorbed in her faith, studying it with a deepened intensity. She once told Pierce that when she learned that the religious state is higher than any other, she was glad her station in life was fixed, for had she been a girl deciding on her vocation, she would have determined to give up everything to God.

One morning on a bright day in January of 1840 she was walking with her children through the convent grounds. Mercer was eight now, Adeline almost five, and John a beautiful golden-haired boy of nearly three. Suddenly to her horror, she saw little John run ahead, stumble and fall into a kettle of boiling maple juice. He was terribly burned and after hours of agony he died in his mother's arms.

Hardly had this sorrow lost the sharpness of its agony when she was called on to make a very different renunciation. One morning as she walked home from Mass with her husband, he stopped suddenly and, putting his hands on her arm, looked deep into her eyes. "Cornelia, I want to be a priest."

She looked at him aghast. "A priest, Pierce — but you can't — you are married."

He hesitated. "I know. But there can be exceptions — if the wife will enter a convent."

There was nothing for her now, she thought, but prayer. She knew she was always willing to follow the will of God. If only she could be sure that this was God's will. Pierce whom she loved — to wish to go from her in this way — and what would become of their two children and another to be born in a few months ?

Years later Cardinal McCloskey spoke of her grief and bewilderment in those days. She had come to him, a simple priest then, and poured out her troubles to him. "Is it necessary," she asked him, "for Pierce to make this sacrifice and to sacrifice me ? I love my husband. I love my darling children. Why must I give them up ?"

Much moved, he could give her no answer. "Wait and pray," he counselled.

In the spring of 1841 her last child, Francis, was born. In September she made a retreat and at its end wrote in her diary, in a steady hand, "Examined vocation. Decided. Simplicity — confidence."

Now she began the work of breaking up her home ; she put away some of her furniture and sold a good deal of what remained. Pierce was to go alone to Rome to get the necessary permission to study for the priesthood, but at the last moment he decided to take Mercer with him to England and put him in school at Stonyhurst, the Jesuit Academy. Cornelia remained with the other children at the Sacred Heart Convent and wrote loving letters to the little son so suddenly torn from her. "I bless you, my dear boy, as you go to your bed, as if I were close to you and you have only to whisper to your Guardian Angel or put a little cross on your forehead for me."

Pierce wrote her from England that he had a temporary position through the Earl of Shrewsbury to act as tutor for a young English lad with whom he was travelling to Rome via Belgium, Fribourg, Munich, Milan, Ancona, and Loreto, and he was glad of it, for it would bring in a little money for them both. Later he wrote that he had at last reached Rome, and laid his petition before the ecclesiastical authorities. He was told that his wife would have to come to Rome also before anything could be done about his case. So he returned to the United States to get her. She came with the children from Grand Coteau to Philadelphia to meet him and they set sail in August 1843.

After some months in England and France the Connollys took an apartment in Rome. It was a queer life for Cornelia, for she had her husband with her again, and yet they were always on the verge of lasting separation. They went out into society, although she felt that such interests should really be ended for her. And then, too, she had the uneasy feeling that Pierce's own attitude was not exactly that of a man who was about to forsake domestic life and worldly honors.

In 1844, the Pope suddenly put an end to all their waiting, and Pierce learned that he was to be given minor orders immediately. It was decided that Cornelia should enter the Convent of the Sacred Heart, where Ady was already going to school. But she was to be merely a postulant, so that she might have little Frank with her as long as he needed her. In Holy Week Pierce received the tonsure; the document permitting the separation of husband and wife had already been executed and signed.

Mercer was to stay at school in England and spend his holidays with his father, and to see his mother occasionally.   Ady would remain with her mother in the convent until her education was completed, and Frank would stay there until he was old enough to go to school.   Cornelia, who had agreed to everything proposed to her, now entered the convent.   When its gates closed on her, the loneliness and seclusion affected her like death.   For the first time she fell really ill, and this after a retreat where she had expected to find peace at last out of pain. All she could feel was repugnance and desolation.   Her diary shows her hopelessness of the future, yet she knew there was no retreat for her into the past.   "I offered that which the others understood.   My soul sleeps.   At the Mass I sang half asleep.   I had some stray thoughts about the children.   Father de Villefort thinks Frank ought to stay with me until he is eight years old.   I think so too."

On June 18, 1845, she made the solemn vow of chastity which was required before Pierce's ordination could be complete.   Four days later he was made subdeacon and a month later he was ordained a priest.   When he celebrated his first Mass, Cornelia sang in the choir and Ady watched from a pew.

For months Cornelia waited to make sure of her own future.   She loved the nuns with whom she lived, but she did not feel sure that her future was to be with that congregation, although she knew no other nuns nor was there

any other order she wished to enter.   Carmel drew her
— but that was out of the question with little Frank to
consider.

Suddenly the question was settled for her.   Cardinal
Wiseman was very much interested in Catholic education for English girls, and, with the Earl of Shrewsbury,
he interested the Pope in the matter, suggesting that
Cornelia Connolly would be an excellent person to take
up this work.   She would have preferred beginning such
an undertaking in her own America, but she yielded to
their wishes.

There was now little money left to either of the
Connollys.   Pierce wrote home to his brother that his
"blessed angel of a wife" and the little ones had to travel
in servants' places on the steamer — "and the hat I now
wear is the only one I have worn winter and summer for
more than two years."   He added he had been given an
appointment by Shrewsbury as his private chaplain on
his estate in England.

Cornelia Connolly began her life as a nun in a strange
way — in England which she did not know at all, with
no friends to tell her what to do, and with two young
children to care for.   But that last problem Pierce solved,
as he loved to solve problems.   He suddenly decided
these children were also to go to boarding school.   He
gave no explanation except that thus he could see them
oftener.

A lay sister, who had come to join Cornelia, said later
that during those days she watched her superior as she

would a saint, so gentle, so patient, was she and yet it
was so apparent that this final loss was almost impossible
for her to bear.

A letter to Mercer at Stonyhurst, a gay mother's letter,
carried sorrow between the lines. She wrote to him
about the other children at school now, just as he was.
"Mrs. Nicholson, the headmistress, says Frank has cried
only once since I left him. And dear little Ady is so
happy, so very happy."

Meantime with the aid of several priests Cornelia was
writing a Rule, as she had been asked to do. The name
she had decided on for the new institute was "The Society of the Holy Child Jesus." From Maryvale Father
Newman, deeply interested in her foundation, sent her
a convert friend of his, Miss Bowes, and several young
girls came as lay sisters. In the meantime Bishop Wiseman had found a convent for them. But when Mother
Connolly saw it, she was overwhelmed. It was so much
larger than she had expected. "But this is not Bethlehem," she said, sadly.

Realizing, however, that the Cardinal had done his
best to give her good accommodations, she put aside her
fears, and set to work with her aids to light fires and prepare an altar, so that when Cardinal Wiseman came to
bless the building and to install the Blessed Sacrament
in the chapel, he found a scene of order and repose.

Mother Connolly was thirty-seven now, her youth
well past her. Her face had a calm and gentleness that
showed the soul within. She worked as hard as any of

the small group with her. She taught the cook how to cook; she taught the little postulants how to sew and clean and paint. Her cool low voice was an inspiration to the girls and women who worked with her. "Her words used to sound sweet and prayerful," said her first lay Sister, "and from the very first she taught us how to live with and in the Holy Child."

The Sisters opened a day school for girls and before the year was out there were two hundred girls to look after. Then a boarding school for young ladies was begun. And at the end of 1847, Mother Connolly made her perpetual vows according to the Rules set up for the Society and was installed as Superior.

During the next years she faced many difficulties. There was trouble between parish priest and convent chaplain and there was the insufficiency of money for so large a project as hers. To settle the last Dr. Wiseman then suggested the transfer of the community to a smaller place — Saint Leonard's at Hastings — and in a short time this was done.

But now another difficulty arose. This was the attention which the Reverend Pierce Connolly began to bestow on the Society. No doubt he was bored and restless, since as private chaplain he had little to do and was not in a position of any authority. And no doubt the kindness and the interest shown him by the Pope when he entered the Church had led him to think he would go higher in ecclesiastical preferment — an opinion which the Earl of Shrewsbury, his patron, no doubt

shared.  But Pope Gregory was dead now, and the new
Pope was not interested.

He began to write letters to the convent, suggesting
as chaplain a friend of his.  This request was granted,
since the priest seemed an excellent choice for the post.
Then suddenly one day Pierce himself appeared at the
convent.  He was told his wife could not see him and it
would be better if he did not repeat the visit.  Not used
to being thwarted, he began to write her letters full of
advice regarding the management of the convent, and
talking as if the whole foundation were his doing.  And
then, as suddenly as before, he took the children from
their schools and departed with them to Italy, refusing
to let their mother know where he had taken them.  She,
of course, could do nothing about it, unless she went
after them in person, which, in the light of later events,
was evidently what her husband had hoped she would do.

Mother Connolly learned that Pierce was in Rome,
trying to have the Rule of her society changed, and at the
same time posing as its founder.  He wrote a set of new
Rules which he presented to Propaganda for approval.
That Office promptly sent them to Dr. Wiseman.  In
the late spring Pierce Connolly came back to England,
without his children, but with an Apostolic blessing for
Mother Connolly and went to the convent to give it to
her.  This time, when his demand to see her was refused,
he waited for six hours in the convent parlor.  Then he
departed, vowing vengeance.

Upstairs Mother Connolly was praying for help, for

guidance. There was the fate of her children in the balance and on the other side of the scales there was her vow to God.

Her husband meantime sent a letter to Bishop Ulla-thorne. "I am a man," he wrote, "and a father before I am a priest, and my first duties cannot be abandoned. I will never forsake the mother of my children. If the laws of justice and honor cannot be at once enforced by the authorities of the Church I am determined to apply to those of the country." He made several conditions : his wife was to have no communication whatever with Bishop Wiseman or the chaplain he had himself chosen for the convent, and he was himself to have free com-munication with his wife whenever he wished it, as well as personal visits in the presence of their children or some other person.

Bishop Ullathorne advised him that he had no juris-diction over the community, even had he wished to exer-cise it in so extraordinary a way. This Pierce Connolly answered by instituting proceedings in the Court of Arches. He demanded the right to reclaim his wife. The verdict was in his favor and an appeal was at once lodged before the Privy Council. By this time even the Shrewsbury family was offering her their assistance, as was also the chaplain whom Pierce had sent to the convent and whom he was now accusing of villainy.

It was a bad time for a case of this kind to come up be-fore an English court. The No-Popery days were at their height and the Oxford Movement had revived much bigotry. Nevertheless the Privy Council reversed the decision of the lower court. Pierce Connolly's answer to this was the publishing of a series of pamphlets against Rome, claiming that his allegiance to that Church had been a delusion — a culpable delusion, he added. The pamphlets were sold all over England at a shilling, and added to the mass of slander the Church had to bear in the land.

The following year he left England, this time not to return. He took his three children from the Italian schools in which he had placed them and established a home for them. He went back to his allegiance to the Episcopal Church. The Church of England honored his return to the fold by naming him rector of the church at Florence. A year later he wrote to his wife once again, asking her to return to him. She did not answer and there was no more correspondence from him.

She heard little from her children after that. Adeline came to see her once after she was quite grown-up, but all the intimacy was gone and the visit caused only grief. Mercer wrote his mother after he left school and came to see her before he left for America to work there at the age of twenty. It was the last time she saw him for shortly after his arrival she had word of his death from yellow fever. On hearing this news, she lost for once her beautiful serenity. When the Sisters came to sympathize with her, she turned sharply from them. "None of you can understand the feelings of a mother," she sobbed.

By 1851, soon after the publication of the Papal brief

which re-established the hierarchy in England, Cardinal Wiseman asked Mother Connolly for some Sisters to teach in London schools. As she had over thirty in the community now, she was able to send several to him and later in answer to a second request sent five more to Liverpool.

What Mother Connolly did during these years was to reform the education of Catholic girls in England. Her students were taught the usual basic subjects but she believed in a liberal rather than a specialized curriculum for girls ; besides the usual school subjects, she provided lectures on philosophy, geology, art, architecture, and even heraldry — and some of Mother Connolly's graduates could read the Gospel of St. John in the original Greek.

Her chief contention was that Catholic girls must be taught to take their place in society and to be a part of the world they lived in. At first her ideas and innovations hindered the growth of the School but later they became so highly regarded that they became a part of the educational system of other schools.

She believed in trusting children and in giving them a certain amount of freedom, and she saw the value of attractive clothes. At one time the school uniform was a silver gray trimmed with velvet.

She lived her life for the children in her schools as earlier she had lived it for her own children. When the boarders were in bed, she used to walk through the

dormitories and make a little cross on each child's forehead, as she had once done with her own boys and her
little daughter. Once a rather tactless nun asked her if
the sight of the children did not remind her of her own.

"The thought of my children never leaves me," she
said gently.

One day, shortly before his death, Cardinal Wiseman
came to see the school. He remembered how twenty
years ago he had told Mother Connolly she was the person for this much needed work. Now he looked about
him at the buildings, the children gathered about, the
many nuns, and the beautiful woman who was their superior. "Reverend Mother," he said, "you have realized
the desire of my heart."

In 1862 the widowed Duchess of Leeds, a granddaugh-
ter of Charles Carroll, came to St. Leonard's for the sea
air, and later made her home at the Convent. It was
she who introduced the subject of a foundation in the
United States, a proposal that brought joy to Cornelia
Connolly's heart. After all, though she had established
her foundation in England as she was bidden, she was
still an American, and to have her Society cross the Atlantic was almost as good as going home herself. Years
ago when she wanted to go to the United States to begin
her work she had been told; "From England let your
efforts in the cause of education reach America."

The Duchess offered Mother Connolly one hundred
and fifty acres of land in Pennsylvania for her first house.

Her agent had written her that there was a frame mansion on the property, together with fruit and garden land. The Catholic church was near at hand.

In 1862 the Bishop of Philadelphia visited St. Leonard's and it was decided that several sisters would go back with him. No doubt Mother Connolly would have hesitated to send them had she known what they were going to find, for the mansion turned out to be a rickety old house in such bad condition that the English Sisters had to work for weeks before they could open a school. They nearly perished in a winter so cold that the wine froze in the chalice at Mass. Once they sold a pair of their shoes in order to get something to eat. Of all this they wrote nothing home, but Father Carter, who knew the conditions, wrote to Mother Connolly that they were living in a shanty worse than the cow houses of England and making an effort "worthy of the early Christians." He suggested they go to Philadelphia to help with his schools there, and Mother Connolly promptly authorized the move. The next year Father Carter bought an old Quaker Academy offered for sale at Sharon Hill in Delaware County and turned it over to them, sending to them children in need of country air and food.

In 1867 the Foundress herself crossed the ocean for the first time since her long exile to visit the two convents of her Society. She stayed only five weeks, and went back to none of the scenes associated with her earlier life, although urgent messages came to her from Grand

Coteau where she was promised a warm welcome. Several of her relatives came to see her and two of her nieces went back to England with her to be educated in her school.

She returned as quietly as she had come. Perhaps she wished to set an example of religious detachment for her Sisters. And perhaps she did not dare, even with all the discipline the years had given her, to stir up the past.

The Rule under which the community lived had never received official approbation from Rome. This had at first been postponed because Pierce Connolly's interference had made Rome apprehensive about the community, and because the authorities wished to wait until matters were more firmly settled.

In 1869, when Mother Connolly went to Rome to ask for this approbation, there had been a great growth in the community. Then it had been a single small house. Now there were foundations not only at St. Leonard's, but at Mayfield, in London, in Preston, in Blackpool, and at Sundridge in Kent, and there were two houses in the United States.

Instead of the answer she had expected, several changes were suggested for the Rule, some of which she was forced to accept against her will. When she returned to England her news almost caused a schism in the Society, so strong were the objections to these changes. Worst of all, the Bishop, instead of aiding her with what she wished, wrote out an entire new Rule for them — one which was even more displeasing to the Sisters than the changes suggested by Rome.

However, she persuaded them all to try it out for the three years which the Bishop wished. There had been such docility to his wishes shown that when in 1877 he called a General Chapter, he was amazed to learn for the first time how much his Rule was disliked. Each Sister in turn voiced her feelings and there could be no misunderstanding of the matter. They felt that at last now, seeing what unanimity there was among them, they would be able to return to their own beloved Rule. The Bishop promised that he would reconsider that matter, but when the decision came there was more disappointment, for he had merely made a few revisions and suggested they try this amended Rule for another three years.

The last foundation made by Mother Connolly personally was in Paris in 1867. She considered this as one of great importance for her Community — "not," she explained, "so much for the good we shall do the children here, though that will be important, if we introduce in our school the teaching of the Holy Child, but there will be a great benefit for ourselves from the contact with the French Church. Here we shall gain more than we can give." She had hoped for a Novitiate House in Rome, so that the truly Roman spirit might pervade their Society, but a house in Catholic France delighted her almost as much.

When she came home she paid a visit to each of the English houses, all still depressed from the disappointment about the new Rule. "Temporal matters," she told them, "are nothing to worry about." It was her last visit to the houses except the Novitiate at Mayfield. From there she went home to St. Leonard's, happy but very weary.

From this time on she resigned herself to an inactive life. Her infirmities were increasing, and during the next year she became a semi-invalid, and much of her time was spent in a bath-chair. Her happiest hours were during recreation time when her novices walked about her as she sat reading or wheeled her chair to a place where she could best see the sunset.

She died in the spring of 1879 after a long illness. During her last weeks she was disfigured by a terrible eczema which covered even her face. But just before her death the Sisters were amazed to see that the marks of the disease had passed away and that her face had again all the spiritual beauty, the delicate color, the gentleness and sweetness they had known for so many years.

She was seventy-three years old when she died. Behind her lay forty years of spiritual work. She had taught hundreds of women to live a life in Christ. She had taught and trained thousands of girls, either through herself or through her Sisters. She had raised the standard of Catholic education immeasurably. She had loved and served God ever since the long ago day when Cornelia Connolly had promised she would do that, had promised it almost against her will, hoping the sacrifice would not be asked of her. But it was asked and met and kept through the years.

She died with two great sorrows on her : her own children were still outside the Church of their baptism, and her religious children were still deprived of the Rule which they loved.

But in 1888 the Rule was restored to them for a five year trial and in 1893 Pope Leo the Thirteenth commanded a decree of final approbation to be published. And after the death of her father, Adeline returned to the practice of her religion and lived a life devoted to good deeds, dying at last from a disease contracted in nursing a destitute woman.

Many praised highly the work of Cornelia Connolly, and extolled the courage and steadfastness she had shown all her life, but perhaps one of the deepest appreciations came from a woman who had known her since the early days of the community. "She would kneel for hours," she wrote, "perfectly motionless on her prie-dieu. I used to watch her and wonder if I should ever be able to pray like that. You could feel her days were spent in the presence of God. Even the small children at the boarding school believed her to be a saint. And with it she was always so simple."

# THE PAULIST GROUP

ISAAC THOMAS HECKER [1819–1888]
AUGUSTINE FRANCIS HEWIT [1820–1897]
FRANCIS ASBURY BAKER [1820–1865]
CLARENCE ALPHONSUS WALWORTH [1820–1900]
GEORGE M. DESHON [1823–1903]

*"In essentials unity; in
non-essentials liberty; in all
things charity."*

As a rule the man who founds a religious community
or congregation has most unusual qualities of mind and
soul. As time goes on he draws to himself others of similar qualities, but his first associates are ordinarily lesser
men than the founder. In the case of the Congregation
of St. Paul, familiarly known as the Paulist Fathers, this
was not true. Isaac Hecker was the leader, the guiding
figure, but Francis Asbury Baker, Clarence Walworth,
George Deshon, and Augustine Hewit were outstanding
personalities themselves. Divine Providence seems to
have brought these men together. Each of their lives
ran in its own groove until suddenly there was one
groove for them all.

Isaac Hecker was born in lower New York in 1819.
Both his parents were native Germans, although his
father's line ran back to the Dutch Hekers who had been
loyal Catholics. Their own branch of the family had

migrated to Germany and become Lutherans. Isaac's
father had little religion ; his mother, on the other hand,
joined the Methodist church in America and Isaac often
went with her to the "love feasts" which were part of
that sect's religious observances.

At first the family had enough money to live simply
but well. Then came poverty, and at eleven Isaac took
a position in a Methodist magazine office. A year later
he went to work for his two elder brothers who had
started a bakery, and he worked as hard as they, taking
his turn at the ovens, delivering bread from a cart.

Even in those days he used to wonder, as he lay on
the shavings in front of the bake-house oven, or sat watching the East River shining in the moonlight, "What does
God desire of me ? What has He sent me into the world
to do ?" From the beginning he was incurably religious,
but never with the careless deistic faith of his father nor
did he ever feel the appeal of his mother's Methodist belief.

There was bitter poverty in the New York of those
days ; there were harsh men bent on acquiring wealth
no matter who suffered. And many did suffer. Depression years made the bad even worse. The Hecker boys
had always been interested in improving economic conditions for the poor, and with this in mind they joined
the various political reform movements of the day, such
as the Workingman's Party. Isaac was very young for
such things, but he shared his brothers' interests insofar
as he could, getting out handbills for the meetings and

distributing them himself. An earnest sixteen-year-old, he sometimes made street-corner speeches about social justice. He joined forces with a reform branch of the Democratic party which called itself the Equal Rights Party. And every day during the hard depression years he helped his brothers distribute loaves of bread to the poor, for the Heckers not only preached but also practised what they believed.

During this period he met the man who was so greatly to influence his life — Orestes Brownson, himself a champion of the poor and oppressed, who let young Hecker discourse at length about the ideas of Kant and Hegel. When the boy confided in him that he hated trade and felt there was something very different he had to do in the world but that the mere studying of philosophy did not show him the way, Brownson offered a suggestion.

"Go down to Brook Farm," he said. "George Ripley is there, and Theodore Parker often comes over to talk. Dana and the Curtises are there too. Perhaps they can help you."

So Isaac went to board at Brook Farm, where the living was plain, which did not bother Isaac at all, and the thinking high, which was what he wanted. Since everyone at the Farm did some sort of work with his hands, Isaac baked the bread for the community. He had been very critical of the product in use when he got there, for the Heckers were extraordinarily good bakers and by this time Isaac was an expert at his trade.

He worked in the kitchen, a baker's cap on his head, his hands kneading busily, stopping only now and then to turn a page of the volume of Hegel he had propped up in front of the board.   Often he shared his ideas with Mrs. Ripley who was ironing or scrubbing, and sometimes Ripley would come in from milking and talk philosophy with him.   At that time Isaac was also reading the Church Fathers, and the kitchen often echoed with the sound of argument, especially if the Curtises or young Charles Dana came in.

Talk was good at Brook Farm and Hecker enjoyed it. But before long he felt uneasy.   The life was pleasant and seemed full, but at its core he sensed an essential emptiness.   Something was wrong despite the learning and the work and the good fellowship.

Not far away Bronson Alcott had started a much more stoic community at Fruitlands.   Hecker resolved to try life here but his dissatisfaction with it was even greater than with Brook Farm, and as an experiment in living it too seemed a failure to him.   The talk was on so high a level it tapered off to nothing.   He noted that Mrs. Alcott and the girls did all the work while Alcott and Lane discoursed.   Despite the farm's name there was hardly any fruit to speak of, and Isaac lived practically on apples and a bit of bread.

He went back to Brook Farm, and the warmth of his welcome almost persuaded him to stay.   However, he did not remain ; instead he went back home for a while, but now he found it impossible to take any great interest in the work that so engrossed his brothers. One thing he was sure of : whatever he might do in the future, he ought to have more education. He decided to go to Concord, and tutor in Latin and other subjects with Mr. Sanborn who had a school for boys there. This plan he carried out, and while in Concord he boarded at the house of Mrs. Thoreau and had long talks with her son Henry and with Mr. Emerson who lived down the street.

Nevertheless he soon realized that he wanted something more than these men seemed to have in the way of faith. They were humanists really, very good ones too, but they were wary of being lured into any religious denomination, having still a feeling of joy and release at their escape from Calvinism. He wanted more than humanism — of that he was sure. He began examining all beliefs — Episcopalian, Congregational, Methodist, even the Mormon. But none of them seemed right and necessary, even though he saw that much in them was better than the transcendentalism which had earlier absorbed him.

Through pragmatic German philosophy, through the semi-mystical dreams of the transcendentalists, Isaac Hecker was reaching some sort of goal at last. In April 1844, he wrote in his diary lines which showed that the shadows around him were beginning to go. "I have been groping in darkness, seeking where Thou wast not and I found Thee not. But O Lord, my God, Thou hast found me — leave me not."

At about this time he discussed his spiritual situation

with Brownson, who after many attempts at joining various sects, was looking deeply into Catholicism and was getting closer and closer to the Church. His talks with Brownson impelled Hecker to consult a Catholic priest, but unfortunately he went to the wrong person for one of his mental make-up — to Archbishop Hughes of New York. The Archbishop was a man to whom "authority" was the chief thing in the Church and who considered individual talent of rather minor importance to the Faith. Hecker was willing to be governed by the most rigid discipline (he had disciplined himself for years) but the Archbishop's attitude seemed to him to emphasize the common suspicion that the Catholic Church was "an Italian mission," a Church foreign in its concepts, incompatible with American ideals.

Then came a letter from Brownson saying he had decided to enter the Church. He counselled Isaac to do the same thing : "There is no use resisting. You cannot be an Anglican. If you enter any church it must be the Catholic. There is nothing else."

It was the sort of categorical statement that Hecker needed. Next day he went from Concord to call on the Bishop of Boston, Bishop Fenwick. Here he found a very different man from Archbishop Hughes, one who was both a student and a philosopher, and who quickly appraised the young man with whom he had to deal. Hecker's objections vanished. He went back to Concord to consider definitely the step he was sure he would take.

Emerson, who knew of the young man's interest in Catholicism suggested visiting the Shaker community in an effort to divert his attention from the Romans. But in his diary Hecker wrote : "We shall not meet each other, for I can meet him on no grounds but those of love. We may talk and reply and talk again." He knew that one period of his life was over, and that neither Emerson nor even Thoreau could confuse him now. He had gone another, and a longer, step on the journey toward faith.

On the first of August, 1844, he was received into the Church in New York by Bishop McCloskey. His family was not unduly disturbed by his new allegiance, for they wanted most of all to see Isaac satisfied. His mother calmly continued her allegiance to the Methodist Church, despite Isaac's efforts to share with her his own happiness. His brother John had become an Episcopalian, but George, to whom he had always been especially close, became a Catholic soon after Isaac entered the Church. In later years this brother was to prove a great financial bulwark for the struggling little community which Isaac founded.

The next year Isaac passed in study and in helping his brothers again. At its end he had firmly made up his mind that he wished to enter a religious order. He had met some of the Redemptorists in New York and thought their simplicity and austerity of life were exactly what he wanted. One day while he was debating about joining them, he heard that several novices were sailing for the Redemptorist novitiate in Belgium the very next night.

He at once set out for Baltimore to see Father von Held, the Provincial of the Redemptorists. He traveled all night, and arrived in breathless haste at Father von Held's door the following morning. Amazed at his impetuosity, but in sympathy with his desire, the Provincial, after giving the young man some hot coffee and asking him to translate from the Latin a page of the *Following of Christ*, gave him permission to join his congregation. One of his questions to Isaac was why he wanted to be a priest.

"I want to bring other people to see the light of the Faith. And I want to work for the conversion of America," Isaac said.

That afternoon Hecker was back in New York, and that evening he was ready to sail for Belgium with the other novices. Two of these young men were converts also. One was Clarence Walworth, son of the Chancellor of the State of New York. He had turned away from his family's Presbyterianism and had studied for the Episcopal ministry at the General Theological Seminary. He had been influenced by Newman, and had read Moehler's *Symbolism*, the book which led so many farther on the road to Rome. With Edgar Wadhams — later a Catholic and Bishop of Ogdensburg — he had become so High Church that the two decided to found a community of their own. It never consisted of more than the two charter members and the community had as its motherhouse the upper story of Wadhams' mother's home. They dreamed together of an Episcopalian monastic pile which would rise some day, of cowled contemplatives and a marvelous religious dreamland. But, mourned Walworth later, "our monastic pile, if it still remains, never was anything but a pile of logs."

"The year of the big scare" — 1854 — saw Wadhams and Walworth Catholics. The former had met Father Rumple of the Redemptorists and suggested to Walworth he do the same, and the result was that Walworth became a novice of that Order.

The other novice was James McMaster, a country lad who by his appearance had excited the amusement of his more sophisticated colleagues at the Seminary when he first appeared there. He was over six feet tall, with a thin face, big nose, eagle eyes, and country ways. But the amusement soon passed as his colleagues had learned that he had an excellent brain and great ability to argue and know what he was arguing about. Though he proved to have no vocation and went home, he was later to become a prominent Catholic editor.

In Belgium something strange happened to Isaac Hecker, some peculiar mental change, and it affected his outer life. He seemed unable to engage in study. He could hardly learn the *Pater Noster* in Latin. During his two student years in Holland and one in England, he could engage in no formal study although his letters

were excellent and logical, and he wrote many. His
spiritual life ran deep and true, and he never lost sight
of one thing for a moment : his desire to become a priest
so that he could aid in the conversion of America. At
last he was simply left to study as he wished, in the Redemptorist house at Clapham, England. Eventually, in
1849, he was ordained by Bishop Wiseman. After this
he went back home with Father Walworth to the Redemptorist house in New York.

Second of the little group who were later to found the
Paulist community was Augustine Francis Hewit. He
was born in Fairfield, Connecticut, the son of a Congregationalist minister whose ancestors were of old New
England stock and who was himself an outstanding
preacher of his day. Hewit's grandfather, James Hill-
house, had been for years a United States senator from
Connecticut. The boy was reared in the Calvinistic
creed of his parents, in a belief in the supernatural and
not in the misty humanism that tormented Hecker's own
youth.

But the Congregationalist teachings did not long appeal to the son of the Hewit house, although he followed
a course in theology at the Congregationalist seminary
in East Windsor, Connecticut. He continued to read
and seek and, being convinced that episcopacy was of
divine origin, he entered the Episcopal Church, but he
began to feel uneasy almost before he was really comfort-
ably ensconced in this new faith.

When Isaac Hecker made his spirited dash to Baltimore, Hewit was studying for the Episcopal ministry there, together with his friend, Dwight Lyman, whose father was an Episcopalian bishop. They lived in the house of Bishop Wittingham, well known for his Catholic tendencies — not Roman Catholic, however, for he had a bitter hatred of that Church.

Under this roof, both young men were at first content, for in that wing of their sect they found a doctrine which was both intellectual and appealing to the heart. They read Newman and the Tractarians; their ritual was, as they believed, based on the "primitive church." Like their bishop, they wore long black cassocks even on the streets. In Catholic Baltimore this did not cause the sensation it might have in Boston or New York. As a matter of fact, they were proud of attention, proud that the cassocks came down to their very heels as they strode along, proud of looking really Catholic. One day their confidence was somewhat jolted when one youngster, playing in the street, saluted them politely and they heard his companion say jeeringly, "That ain't no priest! What are you takin' off your cap for?"

Faithfully from the Bishop's house they went to the church for morning and evening prayers, and with them often went a third young man, also studying for the ministry — Francis Asbury Baker, who lived nearby. He had graduated from Princeton in 1839 and was an ardent admirer of all the ways of the bishop and the Tractarians. Often Catholics on their way to Mass passed the three devoted young men as they went to morning prayers and expressed astonishment at their remarkable piety and began to pray for them. In fact, one of the Cathedral priests used to say Mass for their conversion.

Together Hewit and Baker often visited Catholic churches on their walks through the town. They never went to a Mass, for Bishop Wittingham had forbidden that, but their visits were frequent. Their favorite spot was the Chapel of Saint Mary's College and the Sulpician cemetery behind it. They liked Saint James too, where the Redemptorists were in charge, and they watched the building of Saint Alphonsus' church. They especially enjoyed being greeted by the priests, who no doubt thought these cassocked young men were among their own number. "Gelobt sei Jesus Christus," they said with a friendly smile.

One thing especially moved the two — a memorial to a former pastor of Saint James, inscribed simply : "To the good de Moranville."

"You know," Baker said to his friend, "that does more in a few moments to efface from my mind the effect of calumnies I've heard from childhood against Catholic clergy than a volume of controversy could have done."

The two read Pusey and Newman. They discussed a happy future when the Roman and Greek churches would again be united with the Anglican. They read a magazine called *The True Catholic, Reformed, Protestant, and Free.* They heard their church called the

Catholic Church of America. They strictly followed the ecclesiastical year and agreed with their Bishop that it was the Roman church that was really schismatical and all but formally heretical. The thought of joining Rome had never entered their minds, save that some day they might allow her to come in as a chastened sinner.

Baker was ordained deacon in 1845 and appointed assistant at Saint Paul's church in Baltimore. He proved to be an unusually gifted preacher, but he was a man who never enjoyed praise. What he really wanted was to live a life as a religious and he often talked about this ambition.

One day Bishop Wittingham said sadly to his young men, "Newman has gone." Hewit said he felt as if he had heard news of his own father's death. Now the Bishop began cutting out some of the Catholic observances in his diocese. His young men, as a matter of fact, had been going beyond him in their practices, and he was being approached by annoyed members of his church who, alarmed at the "No-Popery" shouts all about, did not want to be included in such denunciations. He began to refuse many of the permissions his young ministers had enjoyed. The cassocks got shorter and then disappeared entirely. The small church within the Bishop's jurisdiction where the rector had allowed full liberty for High Church practices was being deserted by its indignant congregation. The rector's wife finally objected so loudly (seeing their source of income going), that the church was restored to its former purity, with the old marble-topped communion table replacing the intruding altar.

Hewit was at first amazed, and then greatly saddened, when he realized that to his superior the Catholic attitude was one which could be put on and off with a cassock and a few candles. He went on alone, trying to keep on privately with the practices that to him represented truth. But Newman's defection troubled him, for Hewit was primarily a scholar and loved the scholarly way in which Newman wrote. Hewit waited only until the spring following Newman's submission. On Holy Saturday, 1846, he was received into the Catholic Church in Charleston, South Carolina.

During the previous months he had not seen a great deal of Baker, and though he wrote to him several times after he was received into the Catholic Church, the answers from Baker were so strained and formal that the correspondence lapsed. By 1847 when Hewit was ordained a Catholic priest it had ended completely.

"He has spoiled our plans," Baker had told his friend, Dwight Lyman, himself soon to become a Catholic, to whom Baker poured out in letters all his own uncertainty. He wrote that he himself would never follow Hewit; he would stay where he was, for he believed in the "signs of life" in the Episcopal Church and meant to help in bringing them to fruitfulness again. He too had been amazed at Bishop Wittingham's sudden right about face, but concluded it was merely personal weakness, not a deliberate forsaking of the tenets the Bishop held. Baker would stay where he was and strive to make Catholic again the church of his choice and his love. With the years he became a well known minister in Baltimore, at first at Saint Paul's, and then in a parish of his own, Saint Luke's, where he was to remain two years.

Hewit had in the meantime become a priest and a Redemptorist, and in Baltimore on a mission six years later, in 1853, he met Baker again. During the intervening years they had not written or seen each other, but the conversation between them on this meeting gladdened the heart of Hewit, for it showed him how near the Church Baker was. He was a quiet, deeply reserved man, and his confidences to anyone were few, but he told his old friend how he felt : he was quite sure that Hewit and Lyman had been right in going to Rome according to their convictions, but he was himself still in doubt. He had read and read, but he could find nothing in all his reading to make him sure.

One day as he was walking up and down the Redemptorist garden at Saint Alphonsus, Father Hewit was surprised to hear that Baker was waiting for him in the study. In his face was trouble, but also serenity and joy. "I have come to be one of you," he told Hewit.

What had moved him at last were not high sounding philosophical considerations, but the troubles of a parishioner of his. She was dying, and during the last months of her life she had become convinced that the Catholic Church was the true one. She wanted to be received and her family, hoping to turn her from the idea, asked if she would first talk to Mr. Baker.

She asked him, when he came into her room, if there were any reason why she should not be received into the Catholic Church. And he looked at her and could give her no direct answer. "I'm sorry you asked me that," he said, and realized how inadequate an answer that was to give a departing soul.

She smiled faintly. "I see how it is, Mr. Baker — you are in doubt yourself."

He walked out of the house and on his way passed the Cathedral and felt almost compelled to enter it. Instead he went back to his own rectory to think and to pray. A week later, spent with lack of sleep and sorrow, he resigned his rectorship and went to Bishop Spaulding to tell him he wished to become a Catholic. He then came directly to Hewit to tell him that he had come to join them.

It was Hewit who received him into the Catholic Church in the little chapel of the orphan asylum of the Sisters of Charity. Father Walworth, stationed at the Redemptorist Convent in the city, was there, watching with keen interest the conversion of a man already so distinguished in his own sect. No one else was present, excepting the Sisters and the orphans.

Baker's conversion was a sensation in Baltimore, where he was well known and greatly admired. He paid little attention to this, for he was busy studying to be a priest. Three years later he was ordained in the Cathedral, and when next day he chanted a Mass of Thanksgiving, the deacon and the subdeacon were men who had crossed his path earlier — Dwight Lyman and Augustine Hewit — old friends and partners in many sorrows and joys and trials of conscience. Father Hecker, in Baltimore for an approaching mission, was there to see the happy result of all their prayers.

The group of English-speaking Redemptorists had embarked on a busy career of preaching missions. During the first years Father Bernard had been superior in charge, but now Father Walworth was superior. One other man had been added to the group : George Deshon. He was a different type from the others, a West Point man. He had roomed with General Grant while they both attended the United States Military Academy, and after graduating with high honors had remained to teach mathematics. He had reached the rank of captain and was slated for higher promotion, when in 1851 he suddenly resigned his commission, entered the Catholic Church and announced his plan to become a priest of the Redemptorist Order. He was ordained in 1855.

These Redemptorists had before them an almost virgin field. Public retreats had been given by the Jesuits but the mission opened in St. Joseph's church in New York on Passion Sunday of 1851 was the first mission of a regular series carried on systematically by a body of men especially devoted to the missionary work of preaching and teaching Catholic doctrine.

By 1856 most of the group were seasoned missioners.

Calls upon them had increased. They were needed not only in small towns and remote districts but in the crowded cities, where there were masses of Catholics and an inadequate number of clergy. From 1851 to 1858 the corps gave eighty-six missions, and could count almost two hundred thousand communions. The missions were very popular. Once in New York City the missioners estimated at least four thousand people milling in the streets about the Cathedral which was packed to the doors, with people sitting even on the window sills. Many, swept by the tide of interest, were people who had not come to the Sacraments for years. Confessors were badly needed, and sometimes a bishop sat for ten hours at a time in the confessional to help the hard pressed missioners.

Charleston, St. Augustine, Pittsburgh, Cincinnati, Little Falls, Rutland, Saratoga, Utica, Trenton, and many other cities saw and heard the mission band during those years. Sometimes if attendance in the smaller cities was not what it should have been, one of them rode through town inviting the indifferent and the disaffected to come. And sometimes they were saddened by having so many come that they could not hear half the confessions. "The nets are so full," said Father Hewit sadly, "and not enough workers to drag them ashore."

The English-speaking missioners of the Redemptorist Order could look back on work well done. And with equal fervor they looked ahead to the work of the future,

happy in their life under the wing of the ancient Order
they had chosen for their life work.

Then suddenly trouble arose. The entire group of missioners were American born. They had gone on these
missions with no especial purpose involved save the
spreading of the Gospel. Their work was entirely in English, save for those occasions when Father Hecker, who
spoke German well, found it necessary to use this language. But usually the German missions were handled
by other Redemptorists, and that part of the work of the
congregation was of course the larger, for most of the
Redemptorists of that day were Germans and worked
in the parts of the country where German Catholics were
in a majority.

Now the success of the English-speaking missions suggested to them the foundation of a house for English-
speaking Redemptorists if this work were to be extended.
When this plan was presented there was immediate disapproval from the local Provincial and from higher authority too, although many of the American clergy supported the plan, among them Archbishop Hughes of New
York and Bishop Bayley of New Jersey. The little group
was disheartened. How were they to address themselves
to the non-Catholics of America? How could they come
closer to the conversion of America, the avowed aim of
them all, if their plan were refused at least a trial?

It was agreed among the five that Hecker should go to
Rome and lay the cause before the General of the Redemptorists. This seemed a perfectly permissible thing

to do, since even though the Provincial did not approve of the idea, he gave Hecker a letter which testified that Father Hecker was a good Redemptorist, had great zeal for souls, and his superiors were entirely satisfied with him, even though they did not give their approval to the object of his voyage. But an appeal to the Head was allowed by any individual member, and it was with this in mind that Hecker departed.

He reached Rome but had not even a chance to state his case. He was expelled by the General on the grounds that he had taken money to make the trip — which was perfectly true for George Hecker had furnished the funds. Hecker could not believe the news. He fell on his knees before the Superior and begged him to listen to him. When he saw all effort was useless, he left saying sadly, "Then I have lost the home of my heart."

However, he found good friends at Rome. He found that the Italian branch of the Redemptorists disagreed with the German pronouncement. He met Cardinal Barnabo of the Propaganda, who championed his cause warmly. Others rallied round, and the Pope, after considering the case carefully and after several audiences with Hecker himself, dispensed the five men from their vows, thus ignoring the act of expulsion. And it was the Pope himself who suggested that Hecker should now form a group of his own which would carry out the ideas he and the others had in mind. At his last audience with the Holy Father he begged for a blessing before his departure, "so that I may become a great missionary in the United States," and it was most cordially bestowed. He went home knowing he had the sympathy of the Pope and the Propaganda.

He had written home while the matter was pending : "I am acting on the dictum of Saint Ignatius : 'Pray as though everything depended on God. Work as though everything depended on yourself."

He came home weary but jubilant, and, in July 1859, Hecker with Deshon, Hewit, and Baker (Walworth had left them to be a secular priest in the diocese of Albany) drew up the Rule which was to govern the Missionary Society of Saint Paul the Apostle — the first strictly American congregation in the United States, and named for the Apostle to the Gentiles. It was submitted to Archbishop Hughes for approval.

The finances of the entire group were very limited. For a time they lived at the home of George Hecker who gave them his whole house with its private chapel, while he and his family lived in the country. During the winter and spring the Fathers depended for shelter on friends among the clergy and laity, for a time lodging in a boarding house at Thirteenth Street, close to churches where Mass could be said.

By the spring of 1858, arrangements had been made with the Archbishop to establish a house and a parish in New York. By collecting from friends, and by a large gift donated by George Hecker, money enough was ac-

quired to pay down a considerable amount on the land
they had selected, a large plot at Columbus Avenue and
Fifty-ninth Street.

The place chosen was one of rocky fields and small
farms and gardens. Not far away they could see the
foundation stones of the new Cathedral, on which work
had been interrupted because of the Civil War. Central
Park was just being reclaimed from the wilderness; Broad-
way was the narrow Bloomingdale Road, and once a day
the stage toiled past on its way to Manhattanville. As a
matter of fact, Columbus Avenue existed only on paper
and Sixtieth Street had not yet been cut through.

Energetic efforts were now made by the Fathers and
their friends to raise money to clear the ground and begin
a building which was to include both rectory and church.
Circulars were sent out to parishes where the Paulists had
held missions and to others of the clergy, and the result of
their appeal was an amount sufficient to begin operations.
The first answer to their circular and one of considerable
size came from Father Early, President of Georgetown
College.

In the spring of 1859, the Fathers rented a small house
on Sixtieth Street, fitted up a little chapel in it and lived
there in community until the new house was completed.
The habit they had chosen was similar to that of the
students of the Propaganda at Rome, all black, with a
narrow linen collar, buttoned across the breast and held
at the waist with a cincture.

When the Archbishop had approved their Rule it was confirmed by official permission from the Holy See to the Archbishop, who then established the Paulist Institute in the archdiocese of New York, where they had been heartily welcomed by priests and laity alike. In fact they had received other offers of hospitality; the Archbishops of Baltimore and of Cincinnati wrote offering to establish the community in their dioceses ; Bishop Bayley of Newark, was also very anxious to secure them. Offers to give missions came from various parts of the country, but these first offers they had to decline for the work in the parish was as much as the small group could accomplish.

The cornerstone of the new building was laid by Archbishop Hughes on Trinity Sunday, 1859, and a great throng of people attended. All summer and fall the builders were at work, and on the Feast of St. John of the Cross it was blessed by Father Hecker, who had been elected superior by his associates. In the same month the chapel was blessed and Solemn Mass celebrated in it for the first time.

As the Fathers had to be parish priests as well as missioners, they were happy to welcome a recruit in the person of Father Robert Tillotson, an American convert, who had been for some time a member of Dr. Newman's Oratory. He arrived in time to set free three of the Fathers for missionary duty, leaving two to care for the parish. Perhaps they had not a great number of parishioners at first, but the territory covered was large for it reached from

Fifty-second Street almost to Manhattanville. Before
long Father Alfred Young came to them from Newark
and Father Walworth returned to join his friends.

For the next years everyone was very busy. The mission work was actively maintained, and money was collected to pay off the indebtedness on the property and to
build the rectory. When in November 1859 the new
church was opened, all the regular duties of a large parish
were theirs.

"I have worked hard in my life," wrote Father Hecker
to a friend, "but this is about the hardest. However, it
goes. I had a donation yesterday of two hundred dollars
from a Protestant and fifty dollars from another. *Sursum
corda* and go ahead is my cry !"

The growth of the Society was at no time rapid or spec-
tacular. Until 1865 the members devoted themselves to
the work of the missions. In that year they suffered a
blow in Father Baker's sudden death from pneumonia,
at the early age of forty-four. He was an excellent missioner, an eloquent preacher, and the loss was a great one
to the parish as well as to the Society. The members had
been closely associated because they were so few, and
Father Baker's loss was the first in their fourteen years of
missionary life together.

The church was crowded for his funeral, which took
place during Holy Week. There were many Protestants
in the throng, ministers among them, and one Unitarian
clergyman sent a tribute of flowers. The Fathers who
were left found it difficult to summon enough fortitude

to perform the last rites over him, and the celebrant of the Mass was more than once interrupted by his own tears. Father Hewit, his friend since boyhood, his first confessor, his brother in the priesthood, preached the funeral sermon.

In that same week occurred another tragic death ; on Good Friday the President of the United States was assassinated. Despite the flower decked altar and the Easter music, it proved to be a mournful Easter Sunday.

The mission work had been difficult for the small band and now it became an impossibility ; none were given again until 1872, except such as were part of the labor of their own parish. But prior to this time the Paulists had done good work, and hardly a city of any size in the United States and Canada but had heard their preaching. Since their Redemptorist days they had never changed their method must, for, as Father Elliott said later, "It is hard to improve on Saint Alphonsus." And always they tried to give particular attention to non-Catholics and draw them to some of the mission sermons.

Even though the mission work was temporarily put aside, the Paulist church remained the center of missionary influence. And the reputation of the Society was spreading — their great zeal for making converts, the very exact liturgical observances in the ceremonies, the congregational singing which Father Hecker did his best to foster, the male choir in the chancel which sang the traditional Gregorian chant.

Father Hecker himself did a considerable amount of

lecturing.   The priest in each town paid the expenses of
the hall, the lectures were entirely free, and often they
were addressed entirely to Protestants.   Father Hecker
found the halls crowded for such topics as 'The Church
and the Republic' or the 'State of Religion in the United
States,' or 'Why we Invoke the Saints.'   At Ann Arbor
his lecture was attended by hundreds of students.   This
time his subject was 'Luther and the Reformation.'
When Luther's name was mentioned the students gave
three cheers.   Hecker smiled and asked for a fair hearing, which he got ; and at the end he got what Luther had
earlier received — three hearty cheers.

From the beginning the Society had been definitely
American — definitely and intentionally so, and it was
democratic in the wide meaning of that sometimes abused
word.   "So far as it is compatible with piety and faith"
— the words are Hecker's own — "I am for accepting the
American civilization with its usages and customs ; leaving aside other reasons, it is the only way by which Catholicism can become the religion of our people."

This had been Hecker's purpose always — the aim of
his ideas as soon as he had been sure of the work he was to
do for God, and his single aim ever since had been sure :
to show the American people that they could feel at home
in the Church and need not consider it a foreign institution but the church that was the land — the *ultima thule*
— of each man's heart and soul.   "On this basis alone,
the Catholic religion can make progress in our country,"
he said.

An Apostolate of the Press was one dream Father
Hecker had carried through the years and communicated
to the other members of his Society.  While still a Redemptorist he had himself written two books : *Questions
of the Soul* and *Aspirations of Nature*.  Both works had
for their main object the presentation and teaching of the
Church to non-Catholics, proving that the soul's questions
could be answered by the Church and also that the Church
is the only one which answers the needs of humanity.
Both volumes, published by secular publishers, had gone
into several editions.

The various Paulists had all written volumes of sermons
and Hewit had written a life of Baker which was published with some of the latter's sermons.  But what
Hecker wanted was something other than books.  He
decided that one way to stimulate Catholic literary activities was by means of a magazine.  In 1865 he began the
publication of *The Catholic World*.  During its first year
the magazine contained mainly selections from foreign
periodicals, but within a few years American writers filled
its pages.  Hecker wrote many articles for it himself, and
when he went to Rome for the Vatican Council he sent
back his contributions.  Hewit's scholarly prose also appeared frequently, as well as occasional verse from the
more poetical Paulists, and articles on civic matters such
as public schools and temperance.

From the beginning *The Catholic World* was an erudite, informative, and readable publication.  But still
Father Hecker was not satisfied, for the periodical did

not touch one part of the reading public he was anxious
to reach.   In 1866 he founded the Catholic Publication
Society to spread Catholic knowledge by brief tracts and
booklets.   Some of these proved a great success, and one
little four page tract by Hecker himself entitled 'Is It
Honest ?' went into an edition of one hundred thousand
copies.

In 1870 he founded one more publication, a magazine
for children called *The Young Catholic*.   And the following year he was just about to embark on the daring
idea of a first-class Catholic daily newspaper and collected
half the funds for it, when he had to give up the project
because his health broke down.

During the next years he was often ill and the management of the Society was in the hands of the other Paulists.
But he did a goodly amount of writing and kept the super-
vision of *The Catholic World* in his own hands, with the
able assistance of Father Hewit.   He died in 1888, a few
months after the death of his beloved brother George,
without whose moral encouragement and continued
financial aid the Community would often have had difficult days.

His death was mourned not only in his own city but
throughout the country and abroad.   One mourner was a
man named Gibbons who as a youth had heard him
preaching in the South, and inspired by his words, had
decided to become a priest and who, years later as a
Cardinal had been Hecker's close friend.   From England
Cardinal Newman wrote, "I have ever felt that there was

this sort of unity in our lives : that we had both begun work of the same kind — he in America and I in England."

Once in Hecker's later days, a bishop on his way to Rome asked if he had any message for the Holy Father.

"Tell His Holiness," said Father Hecker, "that there are three things which will greatly advance religion. First, to place the whole Church in a missionary attitude — make the Propaganda the right arm of the Church. Second, choose the Cardinals from the Catholics of all nations, so that they shall be a senate representing all Christendom. Third, make full use of modern appliances for transacting the business of the Holy See."

The other three who had been co-founders of the Society outlived their founder by some years. Hewit, always the ablest scholar of the group, became in his later days even more of a teacher than a preacher. He wrote many articles for *The Catholic World* and was its editor from the time of Hecker's death until his own death in 1897. Father Deshon, the practical member and former army man, who was the architect of the new church and had been accused by some of making it look like a fort, outlived them all. He was a gentle, kindly man, but he did occasionally act with almost military precision if a wrong needed righting. It was due to him and his insistent efforts with the city fathers that a very infamous dive which was ready to open on the Bowery never opened at all. He died in 1903 at the age of eighty surviving by three years Father Walworth.

It was a band of stout hearts and good intellects — this group who had followed daily in the steps of the Apostle to the Gentiles. A few years after their founding some-one had murmured that these "Yankee priests" were going to Americanize the Catholic Church. But their work through the years showed that their aim was to change not the Church and make it American, but to change America and make it Catholic. The fact that Father Hecker was invited to speak at the Plenary Congress at Baltimore, that he was sent by the Bishop of Ohio to the Vatican Council as his theologian, that the pages of *The Catholic World* never met with censure through all the years — all these things and many more showed how idle was such a remark.

The actions of the Paulists through the years showed how thoroughly they loved and obeyed the church of their choice and how they had made their own the words of the Apostle who was their patron : "One Lord, One Faith, One Baptism."

As they went about their day's business they had always been too busy to listen to compliments, but Father Camp-bell of the Jesuits, who had known them all, gave a sketch of each man in his sermon at the Paulist Jubilee in 1910. Hecker was tall, erect, robust, with clear blue eyes — "I think in other times he would have made a magnificent martyr," said Father Campbell. Father Baker had a face like a medallion, an ascetic profile, a musical persuasive voice. Hewit was an intense man, though always deeply reserved, and looked like a patriarch, for his hair turned

white early.    Deshon was always kindly and pleasant but
had military fire in his eye when aroused.

One and all they were men who had deliberately turned
their backs on families, to cast their lot with the despised
Catholics for whose faith they had left their gracious family traditions.    When Father Campbell preached the funeral sermon of Isaac Hecker he was speaking of all the
band who began their life in the Church with him.
"Amid the darkness of forty years ago," he said, "a star
shone before the eyes of another watcher and he, like the
kings of old, arose and followed it, keeping ever onward
through doubt and disappointment and defeat till he
found the long sought Christ and laid at His feet the gold
and frankincense and myrrh of his past life."

# JAMES KENT STONE

## FATHER FIDELIS OF THE CROSS
### [1840–1921]

> *"I found it as a treasure
> hid in a field."*

During the eighteen sixties Kenyon College, in the friendly and pleasant little Ohio town of Gambier, had as president a man who doubtless was both the most brilliant and the most troublesome incumbent that office ever held. His name was James Kent Stone, and he came to Kenyon as instructor a few years before he was inducted as President at the early age of twenty-seven.

He came of a family well known in Episcopalian annals. He was named for his grandfather who, as Chancellor Kent, was referred to by the *American Bar Journal* as late as 1921 as the American Blackstone. His father, John Seely Stone, was rector of St. Paul's church in Boston and was once described by a parishioner, Daniel Webster, as the foremost preacher of his time. He had established at Harvard an Episcopal school of theology expressly in order to combat the nebulous Unitarianism then prevalent in New England, and he was the author of works on theology which are still used as authoritative by representatives of the Evangelical branch of the Protestant Episcopal Church.

Kent Stone was educated at Dr. Dix's Latin School in Boston. He read Horace in Latin at fifteen as easily as

he did English ; at eighteen he wrote Latin poetry as
fluently as he wrote English verse. After graduation
from Harvard he was sent abroad to study for a year in
Germany and Italy and learned to speak fluently the languages of both countries. He made the ascent of Mont
Blanc, the youngest person ever to do so and was therefore
made the only American member of the English Alpine
Society. On his return he went back to Harvard for a
higher degree and during that year met and became the
close friend of Oliver Wendell Holmes.

He taught for a while at Dr. Dix's school, but when the
Civil War began he enlisted as a private, steadily refusing
the commission which was offered him.

He was twenty-seven when he was offered the presi-
dency of the flourishing little Ohio college. He accepted
eagerly for two reasons : it would be a great opportunity
to put into practice some of the ideas he held on higher
education, and it would offer a better income than he had
so far had. He needed the better income, for some years
before he had married Cornelia Fay of Boston, and the
young couple had three small daughters to bring up.

President and Mrs. Stone were very happy at Gambier.
The life there was simple and pleasant and the youthful
energy of the new head was, the trustees decided, exactly
what the school had needed. They liked his simple
friendliness too and the lack of Eastern aloofness they
had feared he might have. He was often to be seen
walking along the tree-shaded streets, a small daughter
clinging to either hand, or perhaps wheeling the youngest

in her carriage. He had three reasons for pride, he used to say — his well managed college, his attractive family, and his garden.

Every spare moment was spent in this last named place and though the summer was very dry the townfolk noted that Dr. Stone had the best vegetables in town in his garden, and the small white cottage was always embowered in flowers he had grown and tended himself.

Before the first year of President Stone's tenure of office was over, however, there was trouble. It rose not from any lack of ability, for on this score none found fault with him. It did not come from the students who adored him. In fact, they crowded themselves into the narrowest quarters to make room for the congregation of outsiders who came to hear his sermons. The excellent content of his talks, his melodious voice and his impressive delivery made him outstanding. The trouble came from the Episcopal authorities, for the theological school at Gambier was under the charge of the Bishop of Ohio who held strictly to an evangelical interpretation of Episcopal doctrine. When Dr. Stone was elected, his theology seemed sound enough ; there was the reputation of his father to make it even sounder, and the reverberations of the Oxford Movement had until then provoked no faintest echo in the halls of Gambier.

But one day during an argument he was asked how he would defend the theory of the validity of the position of the Anglican church if ever he were called on to do so. He answered that he reconciled it with Catholic unity on the basis of primitive Christianity as it had been before it had been confused by Roman influences and corruptions which were an incubus it had to throw off, thus saving its spiritual life. But even in this mild doctrine the Bishop had evidently sniffed a whiff of incense, and he began to fear lest the young man might be heading the Bishop's flock to the wrong fold. He began to study the young president's sermons with great care, and so did others to whom he had confided his fears. Before long criticism arose about these sermons, and also counter criticism from President Stone's friends, especially the student body.

Louder and louder grew the murmured complaint and dissatisfaction, until Mrs. Stone was writing unhappily from her pretty white cottage to her relatives in Boston, "I cannot predict our future."

President Stone's first year at Kenyon was hardly completed before he was all but forced to resign. But almost immediately he was invited to become President of Hobart College at Geneva, New York, another Episcopalian college. This was to prove a far happier place for him, for there was no bigotry such as he experienced at Gambier. In fact, the Bishop of New York was quite High Church in his leanings. Dr. Stone's sermons were received quietly and there was no contradiction of his views.

Life began to run smoothly again in the Stone household when another blow came. The young wife was taken suddenly ill and within a week her distraught husband was left with three small girls to raise alone. He did his best, however.   He installed a good housekeeper and a nurse in his home and prepared to continue as best he could when another blow came.   But this one he was dealing to himself.

He had felt for some time a certain uneasiness about the doctrines of the Episcopal Church and a sense that things were wrong about that communion.   For a year or more he had been disturbed but not enough to make a move.   Then one morning he wakened early, and lay listening to the sounds of birds twittering on the campus and watched the sun stealing over the window ledge, as he waited for the rising bell to ring.   Suddenly into his mind, and not as the outgrowth of anything he had previously been thinking, came the thought, "What if the old Roman Church is right after all ?"

He was terrified.   He pushed the thought aside and all that day he strove to forget it.   But from that morning he knew no inner peace, and from that morning the feeling grew in him — a feeling that was almost a horror from which he sought to escape — that he could no longer remain in the Episcopal Church.   Yet this was the church where his grandfather and his father held such honored places as layman and cleric, where his mother dwelt so happily, whence his own advancement had come, and where were his friends, his prospects for a future for himself and the children now doubly dependent on him.

He read and pondered, and the more he did so the more sure he felt that authentic Christianity was not to be found outside the Roman Catholic Church.   Telling no one of his family or his close friends of his trouble, he waited until the end of the college year, and then sent in his resignation.    It was described by the trustees in their report as "a stunning blow."

He wrote to his parents, explaining that he had resigned because he could not continue to preach a doctrine of whose truth he was no longer fully convinced.   He sent the three little girls to the Fays temporarily while he himself went to Madison, a small town in New Jersey, where he lived alone through the next months, asking himself questions and either working out answers in his own mind or gleaning them from books.

He knew nothing of the Catholic Church.   During his year abroad as a student he had visited Rome.   He had seen Pius the Ninth at a ceremony during Holy Week and he had visited the Franciscan Monastery at Fiesole, but these things had held for him merely a tourist's interest and his letters home described them with no more emotion than if he had seen a government function or a beautiful sunrise.

But during his year of decision in Madison one thing had moved him, and that was a letter sent out to the world by that same Pope whom he had viewed so disinterestedly in person some years ago.   The letter urged those outside the fold to consider following the path which Our Lord laid out for them all and to return to Catholic unity. Something in that letter caught the bewildered young man and found a response in his heart.   For one thing it served to show him that there were evidently realities

which others were able to see but which were withheld
from his own eyes. And he saw how, there in his retreat,
he was doing the very thing he had always cautioned his
students against : he was considering all the objections
against Rome instead of considering direct arguments for
the Faith.

He put aside arguments for a time and thought seriously
of his future if he followed the road that led to Rome.
He considered the losses involved — the cherished opinions of the men whom he knew, the hallowed associations,
his useful and good position in his own world, the fair
hopes and plans he had for his future — his again if he
wished to reclaim them. He thought of the grief he
would rouse in hearts that were far dearer to him than
mere hopes or plans.

On the side of Rome there seemed absolutely nothing
for him. He smiled sadly when he remembered how people had spoken to him of the fascination of "Romanism"
and the duty of resisting its seductive charm. "Ah, dear
souls," he wrote in his diary, "what do you understand of
the anguish of a heart that is called to give up all for
truth ? No, on the side of the Church of Rome there is
absolutely nothing — unless it might perhaps be some
attraction lurking in the very completeness of the im-
molation."

He felt himself groping among ruins. His house had
suddenly fallen to pieces about him. Methodically he
began to write down all the arguments he could find, on
one side and the other, and he began to see that those he

had gathered against Rome were mostly those of people close to him. He was afraid he had agreed to these arguments as truth mostly through a fear of hurting those who loved him and even from a reluctance to shut himself from his future career as a teacher.

An inner logic kept relentlessly telling him what he was hoping he would not have to admit : that there was only one Church which, on examination, bore the marks of a Kingdom of Heaven on earth. "I found it," he wrote later, "as a treasure hid in a field — the same field I had wandered in for years and where I had often tramped it under my feet, and when I had found it I hid it, scarce daring to gaze on its splendor and crying as Saint Augustine cried, 'Too late, alas, have I known Thee, oh, ancient and eternal Truth.' And then for joy thereof I went and sold all I had and bought that field."

But "to sell" was not easy. While still at Madison he wrote many letters to his parents trying to explain his position. "What can I do to make your sorrow less ?" he asked them, and knew neither he nor they had an answer. But in one way Kent Stone found his path an easier one than that of many converts. He held and kept the love of his parents, both of whom tried hard to understand what this beloved brilliant son of theirs was trying to tell them in his letters. They failed to understand but they never failed him in their love.

Before the year was over he took his children from their grandmother's home and established them in a convent of the Sisters of Mercy at Manchester. He listened patiently to his mother-in-law's objections and entreaties but he felt that, if this Faith was to be his, it must be theirs too, since his children were too small to choose for themselves and were in his keeping alone. Ethel, his second daughter, the delicate one of the family, died of pneumonia at the convent, and Mrs. Fay was bitter in her insistence that the child's death was his fault.

The other two girls remained healthy and happy. Dr. Stone sold what possessions he still had and gave the proceeds to the Sisters of Mercy for the girls' care. He meantime had come very quietly into the Church and was now hard at work on a book which would explain his action, and at the same time he was studying intensively for the priesthood. He planned to call his apologia *The Invitation Heeded*, basing the title on his own response to the Letter of the year before, the plea for Christians' reunion which Pius the Ninth had sent out to the world.

When published it was hailed as a masterly presentation of the papal position, not only by American reviewers but by the *Tablet* in England. It was in the main the story of a man who had found Protestantism an inadmissible compromise between rationalism and Catholicism, and who at the last found himself in agreement with Cardinal Newman that there was no medium in true philosophy between atheism and Catholicism. "If," he wrote, "this Holy, Roman, Catholic, and Apostolic Church be not the Church then Christianity adds another load to the burden of Mysteries."

He felt a keen desire to become a member of some

religious order and was greatly drawn to the Passionists, but was refused admission because of his responsibilities to his children. Therefore, he entered the Paulist order where the demands were less strict, and he was ordained to the priesthood in 1872.

The small daughters were content and happy in their convent, but their father knew it was not the sort of family life they were entitled to. It made him happy then as well as sad when Father Rosecrans of the Paulists asked him if he would consider their adoption by a wealthy Catholic family in the Far West. There was only one stipulation and that was that he must give up all claims to the children, not only the legal rights but all natural rights as well, for the O'Connors who wished to adopt them felt the children should know as little of him as possible, for the sake of their future happiness and to guard against any divided allegiance.

This separation was the bitterest the young priest was called on to face. Possessions and even parents one could lose; to give up entirely one's own loved children was very different, almost as hard in its way as to lose them by death, as he had his wife Cornelia and his little Ethel. He had felt that lost sensation, when he saw Cornelia in her casket in the little house in Geneva, and Ethel in hers in the convent chapel at Manchester. Now he must give up these other two — almost as definitely and finally, and must do it voluntarily.

That night he took his sorrow to Our Lady of Sorrows, for whom he had a special devotion, and asked for the strength to make the renunciation he knew he would have to make. He told her his greatest grief was that he was giving up his children's love. He could give them up as he had friends and relatives ; what weakened his resolution was that he must give up their love too.

The next day he gave his consent to the adoption. He could do no more for them now. He had given them a Catholic baptism and the name of Mary to each in addition to their own names of Cornelia and Frances. He did one last thing : he dedicated them to the Blessed Mother before he sent them to be the loved children of a new home — a Catholic home, he reminded himself.

He had sold all his possessions for his children's support, but in a rosewood box which had belonged to Cornelia he had kept pictures of the children and of her and her wedding ring and a few bits of her jewelry. That night he resolutely weighted the box with stones, hurried with it to the foot of Fifty-ninth Street, a block from the Paulist rectory, and dropped it into the Hudson River.

After that there was silence and he turned completely to his new life in God. And now, with the removal of the only difficulty that had kept him from the Passionist Order, he left the Paulists for the stricter order to which he had at first aspired. He left the Paulists with deep regret. "Leaving them pressed heavily upon me," he wrote the O'Connors. "It was very painful to leave my dear brethren of that Community."

In religion he took the name of Father Fidelis of the Cross and before long became a valued member of the

Passionist Order. The busy years sped by and he became noted as a preacher. When he was preaching a mission in the Cathedral at Baltimore, President Arthur and members of the Cabinet came from Washington to hear him. He preached at the inauguration of the Catholic University and he was chosen as preacher for the Requiem Mass of Pope Pius the Ninth at Cincinnati and for that of Leo the Thirteenth at Baltimore. He came to be known as the American Newman.

He was twice invited to speak at Harvard and the second invitation he was persuaded to accept. The old college chapel was crowded to the doors, and hundreds were turned away. All were eager to hear the convert priest preach and said they were well rewarded for the discomfort of such crowding. He had been a little fearful about going there again. About this matter he had written, "I cherish the hope of reaching the hub of the universe at last — I wonder will Boston be kind to me." He realized they would when he saw the crowd come to hear him in Appleton Chapel.

He went to South America and built foundations of his order : in Buenos Aires, in Cuba, Panama and Brazil as well as in Spain and the United States. He gave missions to the Negroes and retreats everywhere. His own order gave him high honors, electing him consultor to the General, master of novices, provincial in the United States and later in South America.

When, in 1916, the United States entered the World

War, Father Stone offered his services; at seventy-eight he volunteered as chaplain.

He received word from time to time that his girls were well and happy; and once, ordered by his superior to do so, he had paid them a visit, but it was not a success. He had not dared express his love for them, mindful of the fact that he had given his natural rights to his children away when he had agreed to their adoption.

Very often he had wanted to write another book but there had been so little time for literary work. Then his superiors decided that his first book, written so long ago and in the heat of controversy, needed revising and the incorporating of new material. He decided to call it *An Awakening and What Followed*.

Every day he wrote some pages. His handwriting was still firm and clear; his ideas were as clearly expressed as ever, but he was over eighty now and could write for only a few hours at a time. He knew he must keep on though or the book would not be finished. He walked very slowly who had always taken great strides, and though he still stood erect in his height of over six feet, he had to move with caution. His great luminous eyes held more of patience than any desire to prove or disprove controversy. But he set to work to tell again the story of his life.

Out in the Far West, Frances O'Connor, who had been little Frances Stone long ago, read the new book by Father Fidelis. Until she read it she had never known

how greatly her father loved her and her sister. She
knew he was her father of course, for there had never
been any secrecy about her parentage, but for the first
time she learned how mighty a sacrifice he had made in
giving up her and Mary and following a religious vocation. It was not that he made a long story of it ; in fact
the adoption was not mentioned. But one stanza in
the book told her more than all the years had said.

He wrote of sitting on the beach at Monterey where
he was giving a mission, idly tracing with his finger in
the sand, and suddenly he saw he had written there the
names of his children — and he had not even seen them
for many decades or years. He put the incident in verse
in his book :

> "A name I wrote upon the sand,
>   Where curled the long waves' foamy crest —
>
> \* \* \*
>
> Dear God, in all the empty world
> I seek no home for evermore,
> Nor look for rest till by the shore
> Of death my ship her sails has furled.
> No more to wander and no more
> In all the world to seek for rest, —
> Only to wait, and by the west
> Look wistful toward the unseen shore."

On impulse, not knowing where she could reach him,
she sent her father a letter which followed him around
and finally reached him at Norwood Park, where he lay
very ill — dying, he himself thought.

He read it through, scarcely crediting what he was reading. He read it again. Then he went to the chapel to thank Our Lady of Sorrows who had watched over his love for his daughters for him as he had begged her to do some fifty years ago, and who was now showing him how that love had been safe in her keeping all that long time.

Only a month before he had told Our Lady, now that he saw that life was for him at most a matter of months, how willingly, how gladly even, he had given up hope of hearing from his children again or even knowing if they knew anything of him or cared about him. And now, at the very close of his life, their love was coming to him.

"Our dear Lord," he wrote to Frances, "through His mother gives you to me, as his best earthly gift, unasked for, undreamed of, a gift that more than makes up for all that ever was or ever was lost. I desire no more, I die happy."

"In Our Lord's good time they will know how much I loved them," he had written years before. Now his small prophecy was fulfilled.

His daughter came from California to see her father with no delay, and a few weeks later, with the permission of the Father Provincial, she took him home with her to see his other daughter. In the little chapel in Mary's home he said the Mass of Pentecost. And he sat through the long sunny days in her garden, always in his Passionist habit, his daughters near him, and he knew the added joy of a sturdy grandson who played about his chair, a boy who smiled at him with Cornelia's eyes.

He had hoped to do one thing more before he died : he wanted to have Frances go with him to Cambridge for his sixtieth class reunion. But first he wanted to say Mass on Saint Theresa's feast at the nearby Carmelite convent. He died on the eve of that feast, happy in the knowledge that the love he felt for his children and the love they felt for him had been kept living, waiting for him as his reward at his life's end.

In the Harvard *Graduate Magazine* his death was listed, and the obituary spoke of "an affectionate memory of him — a truly pure and good man."

# IRA DUTTON

## Brother Joseph
[1843–1930]

*"Brother to everybody."*

"Unclean, unclean" — down through the ages comes to us that most terrible of all warning cries uttered by human beings afflicted with the disease most dreaded in any land in the world. In ancient days lepers went their solitary way, shunned by other men and women, forbidden even to speak to a child, and so feared that if their very shadow fell across a man he felt accursed and had to be made clean again.

In the Middle Ages the scourge had spread to western Europe. The leper was still an outcast, and the only difference was that now instead of being driven into caves and holes in the desert, he was declared legally dead, and a Mass was read over him — the leper Mass it was called, but it was really the Mass of Burial. Before banishment from home and loved ones, the leper stood either in an open grave or under a black cloth upheld by four stakes while prayers were chanted for him ; then he was handed a wooden clapper and given various commands — among them that "he must touch no child, not even his own." After that he lived as he could in an isolated cabin, or in later years in a leper hospital.

The care of the leper became one of the greatest charities of the Middle Ages. The Knights of St. Lazarus, composed of crusaders who had caught the disease in the Holy Land, were men who devoted themselves to their fellow sufferers who were destitute. The Benedictines, one of whose rules was that "all who come shall be received as if they were Christ," gave them great help, as did others of the great orders of that day.

As time went on leprosy became less prevalent. In England this terrible plague gradually subsided, until by 1350 there is no record of a single leper in London. But meantime it had invaded the New World, especially the southern portions.

It reached the Hawaiian Islands somewhere about eighteen hundred and spread with terrible speed among the natives, so that fifty years later so many were afflicted that a leper colony had to be established. After much discussion, for no one wanted such a settlement near, the island of Molokai was chosen. It is one of the eight largest islands of the group and about three hundred square miles in size. On two sides and at the back it is enclosed by steep and forbidding cliffs ; the fourth side faces the sea, and since the nearest land is some fifty miles away, there is little chance for the exiles to escape.

In 1874, young Father Damien heard the bishop at Honolulu tell of the crying need for a priest among the lepers in the colony at Molokai. The physical conditions there were almost beyond belief, and the poor outcasts received but little religious aid. The Catholics among the lepers, who composed about one fourth of

the group, had asked for a church, and wood had been
sent for the purpose and a frame building erected, but
only an occasional priest came now and then to celebrate
Mass for them.   When young Father Damien heard
that no one could be found to go to them, he offered to
go himself.   Two hours later he had embarked on a
ship with fifty lepers.

For many years to come he was to fill the duties not
only of priest but teacher, doctor, carpenter, and under-
taker, and he also had the material care of all the lepers,
not only the Catholics whom he had come to serve
spiritually.   He found ninety per cent of the colony
gravely ill.   The lepers had only grass huts to shelter
them, and for many weeks he himself had to sleep on
the ground.   A minimum of medical care was available,
and the spiritual condition of all the lepers was incredibly
bad.

He was not a great scholar from Louvain or Paris but
a simple priest with not much education; nevertheless
he was a man with a compassionate heart and a love for
even the most unfortunate leper in his colony.   He gave
his heart to them — and he gave his life, for after years
of unremitting toil, he contracted leprosy himself.

He was worried now because he realized how much
had to be done and that his own life was almost over.
One day he went down in his old buggy to the landing
port, for a ship had been sighted coming toward the
island.   It was his custom to meet all ships, because there
were usually lepers aboard, and he wanted to greet them

himself, knowing full well the mental condition of these exiles.

There were lepers on the ship, but there was another passenger — a tall man with gray eyes and a quiet face, dressed in cheap but immaculately clean blue denim.

This passenger looked at the short man who stood before him, with the newly arrived lepers grouped about them.   The man's skin was black from years in the tropics ; he wore a queer ill fitting dress, and it was not very clean.   His ears were grotesquely enlarged, and to one who knew the disease it would have been evident that here stood one who was himself leprous.

Father Damien greeted the visitor courteously, but when he heard that here was no visitor but someone who had come to help him, to stay with him, the tired eyes grew bright, and the whole face lightened.   He saw to it that the group of lepers were sent on their trip to the colony, and then he and the man in denim got in the old buggy and the horse jogged along to the colony where the new arrival was to spend the rest of his life.

In the world which he had left the man's name had been Ira Dutton, though some years before he had changed that name to Joseph Dutton.   He was born in 1843 in Stowe, Vermont, of old English and Scotch stock ; the first member of his family had come to New England in 1630.   His father had owned a farm in Vermont and then moved to the town of Stowe and become a maker of shoes.   When Ira was four years old the family moved to Wisconsin where again they lived on a farm.

Ira was a shy, sensitive child, who did not go to school until he was nine or ten years old. His mother read to him the few books in the house — Shakespeare, *Robinson Crusoe*, the Bible, *Pilgrim's Progress*. When he was twelve he worked after school hours on the town newspaper of Janesville, and the next year he supplied for it a column headed "Fun," for which he clipped material from other papers. As the Civil War came nearer, Ira became a member of the local Zouave cadets, and drilled proudly in his wide red trousers and his jaunty cap, not unmindful of admiring glances from feminine eyes.

In addition to these activities and his school and newspaper work, Ira was librarian of the Sunday School at the Baptist Church. When in 1861 he enlisted in the Union Army, the Sunday School gave him in token of his services "a valuable rubber overcoat and a Bible," and promised that the prayers of its members would follow him. As an extra bit of drama, his best girl rushed from the sidewalk as he marched along and gave him her picture. This he carried in every campaign until, in 1864, the Confederates got his baggage and the picture with it.

For four years Ira Dutton fought in the Civil War and his army record was excellent throughout. Just before the conflict ended he was offered a commission in the regular army, but before he could accept it the war was over and he came home.

In the last year of his military service he had met another girl and fallen deeply in love. She was visiting at the post where he was stationed and before she went back to her home in Ohio, they became engaged. His friends in the town tried to dissuade him from becoming involved, telling him that she was fickle and light, and even hinting at a dark past.

He was stubborn in his loyalty. "If she does have the faults you mention I will make her better," he said.

After the war was over he married her, though his material situation was far from rosy — little money, and no job, but he was a bright lad and the future was his. Unfortunately his married life was to prove only one disillusionment after another. The young wife ran up bills which he could not pay. Before the first year of marriage was over, he learned she had been unfaithful to him. He forgave her ; it happened again and he forgave her again. Finally she ran away to New York City with another man. Not until fifteen years later did he divorce her.

During the next years he worked at various jobs, especially in the War Department where he stayed for years, his work mainly the adjusting of claims in the South, the identification of dead soldiers, and the aiding of discharged soldiers who were physically handicapped. He began, with no home life to hold him, with only disappointment behind him, to lead a gay devil-may-care life, and to drink heavily. His friends were worried for fear the habits he was forming would wreck his life. But on July 4th, 1876, he made his own declaration of independence : he would drink no more from that day on. And he kept his word. He also began to abandon his gay life, and the gay times gave way to seriousness. Aghast, one of his friends reported that Ira was reading a Catholic catechism !

No doubt he found the catechism among the books left in his room by his landlady, Mrs. Sullivan, who kept the hotel where he lived in Memphis, and who used to put literature of a pious kind in all her lodgers' rooms. At all events, Ira Dutton was received into the Catholic Church in 1883, in the fortieth year of his life. He paid up all his bills before he entered, and immediately after he changed his name to Joseph in honor of the Saint whom he had grown to love.

His whole life was changed now. "I had determined," he wrote later, "to spend the remainder of my life in penance for past wrongs, to find some work where I could be helpful and do my best for all." Late that same year he dropped entirely from Memphis life and no one knew where he had gone. His friends were amazed, for he was at that time fairly successful in his business.

They could never have imagined where he had actually gone. He was knocking at the door of the Trappist monastery at Gethsemane, Kentucky, and asking if he might stay there. He became a lay brother, one of the men who took no vows, but who worked in the fields and in the buildings of the monastery. No doubt the title "Brother," which came to him later, dates from this period of his life ; but he never was a lay brother in the

real sense of the word.  He was, as he himself put it,
"a common everyday layman."  He always signed his
name merely "Joseph Dutton," and added that the only
title he wanted and would have liked to add to his signa-
ture was "brother to everybody."

For almost two years he stayed at Gethsemane, and
shared the work and the silence of the order.  He rose
at two with the monks for the first of the daily services
in the chapel; he slept on a narrow pallet with a single
blanket to cover him.  He ate the meager fare of the
monks.  Once, in a letter to his friend George Proctor
in Louisville, he said that he had expected to have to
sleep on a board, so that the hard bed he got was really
a luxury.  He told him about a Trappist burial — in
cowl and with no coffin — and said that when he saw
the impressive ceremony he thought it well worth while
to be a dead Trappist.

When he left Gethsemane it was not because he did
not still love the group or the monastery, but because
he felt that he wanted and could better serve in a life of
action rather than a life of contemplation like theirs.
He started travelling again, and in Saint Louis he met
with a Redemptorist Father who listened to his story
and suggested he come for a time to his congregation's
New Orleans house.

In their library he began to read the newspapers — he
never got away from his interest in newspapers — and
he came across an item about Father Damien and his
work at Molokai.  It was the first time he had ever heard

of the Belgian priest or the work. Immediately he thought, "Could I get in there and be useful?" He sought more information about the island and was given a small book on the subject by Charles W. Stoddard. He got in touch with this author who assured him that he would be very welcome in Molokai and gave him directions for the journey.

But before setting out, he went to Wisconsin to see his mother with whom he had lost touch during the past few years. To his joy, he learned that only a year before she had herself become a Catholic. She was alone now, but happy in her small town and with her new faith, and he felt at rest about leaving her, for he felt that he would not soon come back. He settled his affairs and banked the considerable amount of money he possessed. Then, in a suit of cheap clean blue denim, he set out for Honolulu. He left San Francisco on a sailing vessel and enjoyed the new sensation of a sea trip.

On reaching Honolulu he went to see the Bishop and told him of his intention to go to Molokai. The Bishop, seeing this intelligent American, who was offering to serve without pay — in fact, who had money to help — considered him quite literally a godsend and gave his permission with no delay. After getting permission also from the King of Hawaii and from the Board of Health, he left for Molokai with a group of some fifty lepers. That was in July, 1886, at the point where our story began.

Joseph Dutton found plenty to do in the field he had

chosen. He had promised himself on the boat from San Francisco to "get along with everyone and ask no special favors, and do what I can to help my neighbor. It is my hope never to fail in this." He never did, certainly not outwardly. No doubt the silence and the prayer of the Trappist monastery had been a good preparation for his life work at Molokai.

He learned quickly the rudiments of surgery from the doctor there, for by this time the lepers were receiving a certain amount of medical care. He set in order the disorderly books, for Damien hated that work and paid slight attention to it. Daily he rose at four-thirty, worked all day, and it was often one or two o'clock before he went to bed. The last hour or so he gave to reading newspapers, among them the Janesville paper for which he used to do a column, and which continued to come to him at Molokai until the year of his death. He loved writing letters and this time was often devoted to that pleasant task.

He wrote often to old friends in the States, and twice a year a letter went to the Trappists in Kentucky, usually enclosing a souvenir from Honolulu. Sometimes when he wrote a merely social letter he felt guiltily that he was stealing — stealing time from his work. For that was continually increasing, as more and more lepers arrived on the island. Occasionally he wrote to his correspondents not to be afraid : the disease could not be conveyed by letter. In later years he took time to write a scholarly article on Molokai for the *Catholic Encyclopedia*.

Every day he marvelled more and more at the courage he saw around him — bravery, he often said, much greater than in the war he had been through. He enjoyed the playing of the church organist, and when one day he went to tell him so, he saw that one of the man's hands was so diseased that all that was left was a stump which the organist had fastened to a stick and with which he struck the bass notes.

Brother Joseph — his title was fixed almost immediately — also taught the children, for whom he felt a special compassion, the games he had played as a child. Molokai became very proud of its baseball teams, coached and uniformed by Brother Joseph himself. The one thing that had troubled Father Damien was what would happen to his children when he died. Now he could smile and say, "I can die now. Brother Joseph will take care of my orphans."

Not the least of the gain of his presence on the island was his companionship for the lonely priest. They were very different in nature and in upbringing — the serene brother and the impulsive priest, the one scrupulously clean in the blue denim suits which were his uniform, the other careless of what he wore. Damien knew how different they were in temperament — "but there is love between us," he said. He had urged the volunteer to become a priest. But for this Dutton felt unfit. "That requires a high character and great purity," he said and he evidently felt that his early life had disqualified him. No doubt he greatly exaggerated his past evil deeds, but he had the sort of "extra conscience" the saints have.

Father Damien and Brother Dutton found time, usually late in the evenings to tell each other of their early life. But mostly they spoke of the vision which was the priest's and which now was the lay brother's too. They saw in their minds' eyes the colony covered with buildings, shaded with trees. They visioned a Home for the orphan boys and for the girls and better huts for all the lepers.

At that time Brother Joseph's own home was a small cabin which opened into the sacristy. From his cabin window the view was unsurpassed. The sea wall was fifty feet high and the breakers dashing into caves and entrances made a great noise. Before him as far as eye could see stretched the blue ocean, nearly always as blue as the sky overhead. But he had little time for views. After he served Mass and cared for the church he arranged the medicine room and then began his long job — the dressing of ulcers. He had made this his especial task. "It requires quite a knack," he wrote proudly, "to dress and bandage properly and to know which is needed for which stage." There were about seven hundred lepers there, so these dressings were no small task, for he had only one boy to help him and only one real assistant, a German leper.

By 1887, Father Damien's face was terribly disfigured with the disease. Two years later the open sores on his hands kept him for a time from saying Mass. The sores healed, and when he saw the black skin that rimmed the scars he knew that death was close to him. "The good Lord is calling me to celebrate Easter with Him," he said, and it was during Easter week that he died, in his forty-first year. His grave was dug under his favorite tree and a little garden was planted around it. Brother Joseph frequently enclosed a leaf from the plants in his letters.

It was in that same year that Robert Louis Stevenson came to visit the Island and Brother Joseph showed him over it. They went together to all the dormitories and refectories — dark and dingy, but superficially clean. "It is almost decent here," said Brother Joseph, a bit apologetically, "the Sisters will make that all right when we get them here."

Stevenson stayed on the island for a full week, and the lepers spoke of the look of sympathy on his face. But Brother Joseph had noticed also how ill the visitor looked and prayed for him in the chapel after he had gone away. Stevenson sent the colony some little gifts the following month — a piano, a violin, and a croquet set — but later he was to give them a greater gift. Made angry by the hateful letter of a certain Protestant clergyman at Honolulu regarding Father Damien's morals and manners, he wrote a bitter denunciation of the accuser and a heartfelt defense of the man who had lived and died a martyr at Molokai.

Brother Joseph, in his denim suit, his feet bare, now did the work of them both. He said it was like that of a good housekeeper : it never ended. When a building went up to house the orphans he became manager there and remained so until his death. More and more helpers came with the years. By 1923 the settlement had become completely up-to-date, sanitary in every detail, and the doctors and nurses were adequate for the lepers' needs. A Girls' Home had been built and there were Sisters to care for it, at their head Mother Marianne, who next to Father Damien and Brother Dutton, was the most important worker in Molokai.

During the years Brother Joseph had had various quiet occasions for joy to compensate for voluntary exile from his own country. One was when the Hawaiian Islands were annexed by the United States. Always a patriot, he wrote in his letters home as if his country was a living thing of flesh and blood. Always on his desk was a little flag of the land from which he had exiled himself in the body but never in spirit.

In 1908, Theodore Roosevelt ordered the U. S. fleet which was returning home to sail past Molokai. The man who had been a faithful soldier in the Union Army for four years and for many succeeding years a faithful soldier in the army of pain, stood on the beach of the island surrounded by his leper boys, the American flag waving proudly over their heads. In battle formation the fleet swept past, each ship dipping its colors as it passed the tall figure in blue denim at the water's edge.

In 1916, when he was over seventy years old, Brother Dutton was eager to volunteer for the World War. He planned to ask President Wilson to let a few of the old

men go as independent sharp shooters, perhaps even in
the old blue uniforms, so that the cost of sending them
would be very little.  He tried some army exercises himself, however, before he wrote the letter, and suddenly
realized that he was too old for active service.  So he
turned to other ways of helping.  With the last money
he had in the bank he bought Liberty Bonds at Honolulu
and he sent his only and prized possession — a fine pair
of binoculars — to Mr. Roosevelt, the Assistant Secre-
tary of the Navy.  When the binoculars were returned
after the war, Mr. Roosevelt assured Brother Dutton
that the glasses had seen actual service on a battleship.
Brother Dutton was anxious for the lepers to have a part
in the war effort, for they were all American citizens too.
And they did raise a considerable amount to send the
Red Cross, collecting it by doing chores of various kinds.

One day Brother Dutton received a letter from an
old friend — a correspondent of years — Mother Alphonsa, the Dominican nun who was working for the
cancerous poor of New York.  It had been a long time
since he had seen her eager, spirited handwriting or read
her brilliant sentences.  She had something to ask of
him now, he found : would he perhaps, now that the
leper work was well taken care of by many people, would
he perhaps come to help her — if only for a time ?  Could
he come to New York, perhaps even founding an order
for the purpose, and take care of the cancerous men patients and she would continue her work with only the
women ?  "The doctors tell us no paid orderly is temper-

ate and few of them are kind," she wrote in explanation. And she told him she knew the means would be provided for the work if he would only come.

He looked at the letter for a long time after he had read it through twice.  Then he shook his head in deep sorrow and wrote her that he could not come, and wrote her why, but he told her that his strongest prayers would be for her and her sufferers.

Weeks later her answer came — her thanks, her regret. "Dear great life," it ended, "you dared to become an Apostle, and they always come too close to Jesus to escape His courage, His glorious wounds — may God be with you."

The last years of his life brought him additional honors. He heard that a school in Wisconsin had been named the Brother Dutton School.  In 1929 the Holy Father sent his Apostolic benediction 'to the Venerable Brother Dutton,' and a priest friend in the States told him that "the Holy Father has your radio portrait on his desk." That same year the Hawaiian Legislature voted a resolution of appreciation to the man who had worked for over forty years among the lepers.

During his long life his health had been almost perfect, but by 1928 his sight had become very bad.  And one evening when he went out to get the flag, he had for the first time in his life to sit down suddenly because of weakness.  Pneumonia developed and he himself feared that his end was at hand.  He promised his beloved Saint Joseph that if he recovered he would take care of his greatly neglected correspondence. When he got well he devoted all the time he could spare to putting his papers in order.

He was a little amused about himself and the old age that was finally upon him. "I am sort of an old relic here now," he wrote to American friends, "but still on duty and very happy, almost ashamed to say inclined to be jolly. Often think we don't know that Our Lord ever laughed and my laugh is ready to burst out any minute."

Some months later he was taken to Saint Francis' Hospital at Honolulu. He had not really wanted to leave Molokai but was finally persuaded to do so. As the ship carried him away he looked at his island. It was dim now to his failing sight but that did not matter at all. For he was seeing it with the eyes of the past — a sandy beach — an old horse and buggy — a tired man with the marks of leprosy on him whose eyes had lighted when they heard he had a new helper. To Brother Dutton any sight of Molokai held Father Damien as its central figure. The years since Damien's death were merely the years he had devoted to carrying out Damien's plans and loving Damien's lepers.

In the hospital, in his white hospital robes with his snowy hair and beard, he looked like a saint. When someone asked him if he regretted the troubles he had had and the difficulties of his long life, he shook his head. "I regret nothing but the evil in the world — and leprosy," he said soberly.

He still retained the ready wit he had with him all his life.   When a man spoke of a visitor who had been very rude at Molokai to Brother Joseph and said he should have pulled a picket from the fence and broken it over his head, Brother Joseph smiled the old gay smile and said, "Maybe I should have — but I didn't want my fence spoiled."

In 1931 Brother Joseph died.   The day that news of his death came to Molokai the cliffs echoed with the sound of the weeping and wailing of lepers, as it had resounded years before when Father Damien died.

Brother Joseph's body was taken to the Cathedral where the funeral Mass was sung.   His was almost a military funeral.   The Sixty-fourth Artillery escorted the body from the church to the cemetery; over his casket was draped the flag of his native land.   As the crowd stood silent about the casket three reports broke the silence.   Then a bugle sounded taps over a soldier's grave.

# JOHN BANNISTER TABB
[1845–1909]

EVOLUTION

*"Out of the dust a shadow,*
*Then a spark ;*
*Out of the cloud a silence,*
*Then a lark ;*
*Out of the heart a rapture,*
*Then a pain ;*
*Out of the dead cold ashes*
*Life again."*

The first picture of John Bannister Tabb, taken in 1855 at the age of ten, shows him almost hidden by a large dog. In fact, it was the dog who was having his picture taken and John was merely holding him quiet. But it proved good of them both : the huge dog, the thin determined looking boy, staring straight at the daguerreotyper.

John Tabb's family came from England before 1650. When the first ancestor reached the New World he began buying land, and when he died he left several thousand acres to his son, who left his own son a goodly heritage. The family was very much a part of the Old Dominion — planters, merchants, statesmen, bankers.

John was born at The Forest, an estate long held by the Tabb family. He lived the happy life of a child of well-to-do Southerners, with a mammy who used to show him off as "the ugliest baby ever born in Virginia." He loved her as dearly as she did him, and when she died after he was grown up, he wrote her epitaph :

143

"To her, O Tenderness Divine,
　　Be Thou, as she to me and mine."

His mother taught him to read and write and to say his prayers. He later had a tutor, and some of the children of neighboring estates came to join him and his brothers at their studies. Johnny was not much of a student in those days, but very early he showed great musical talent — so much so that everyone expected he would devote his life to music. Even as a small boy he spent from six to eight hours at the piano.

When the Civil War came his elder brother William went into the Southern army and rose quickly to the rank of colonel. John, sixteen, and Yelverton, fourteen, were considered too young to go. John's eyes troubled him even then, so it is doubtful whether he would have been accepted anyway. But Yelverton ran away and joined his brother's regiment. John's disappointment at being left behind was so intense that his cousin, Captain John Wilkinson, made a place for him as clerk on his ship, a blockade runner.

This ship would creep into the harbor at night to land the precious supplies it carried. Once looking out over the dark water, John eager to be helpful, shouted suddenly to the pilot, "I see a rock. I see a rock."

"Not a damn rock in the State of North Carolina," said the pilot, and Johnny subsided.

Their vessel, originally called the *Giraffe,* but later re-

named the *Robert E. Lee*, had a busy time.  She successfully ran the blockade at Wilmington twenty-one
times with arms and guns for the Confederates.  And
while these supplies were being purchased in various
ports Johnny managed to see a great deal of the world,
since the ship touched at such points as Havana, London,
Dover, Boulogne, and Glasgow.  However, in 1864 the
ship was captured by the United States *Keystone* and
John spent eight months as a prisoner at Point Lookout.
It was a terrible experience and years later, if he saw an
especially wretched looking beggar he would say to himself, "I 've been in worse case than that man."

His health impaired by the prison life, he was lying
one day on his cot at Point Lookout, when he heard the
faint sounds of a flute playing a strange sweet melody, a
haunting air that carried the homesick boy far from his
unhappiness and pain.  He learned later that it was the
flute of Sidney Lanier, the poet, who was also a prisoner
and who had smuggled the instrument past the prison
guards by hiding it up his sleeve when he was captured.
After John met Lanier, the prison became a happier
place, for the magic flute and conversations with a kin-
dred spirit about literature and poetry made him forget
his misery.

In 1864 John Tabb, not quite twenty, was exchanged
as a prisoner of war.  He stood on the road that led
to freedom and felt he was in the Kingdom of Heaven
itself.  He started for home and on the way was able

to travel with his brother's regiment for a while. And once he saw General Lee himself, standing quite alone and very still.

Like many Southern soldiers he came home to desolation and ruin. The lovely plantation was a waste. The acres of fields were unplanted and there were no green shoots of growing corn, only buds of wild vines. The household was equally bereft. Linens had gone to make bandages; brass had gone to make cannon; silver and other stores had been sold or used up over the years and had not been replaced.

While on the *Robert E. Lee*, John had met Major Ficklin who was interested in the boy's musical talent. When he learned of his immediate need of training in order to earn a living, he took John to Baltimore for a year and paid for his music lessons. Then, the Ficklin estate having gone bankrupt, he had to give up his aid, and the young man accepted a position as teacher in St. Paul's Episcopal School in Baltimore. It was close to Mount Calvary, a very ritualistic Episcopal church in the city, where the rector celebrated "Mass" and wore a biretta, and where candles flamed on an altar and even, it was rumored, confessions were heard. The rector, the Reverend Alfred Curtis, a man who was looking Romeward even when young Tabb first met him, became his great friend.

In 1870, Tabb got a better position at Racine College in Michigan, but he was not satisfied with the work he was doing. After long pondering, he entered the Episcopal Seminary at Alexandria, Virginia. It was at the very time that Alfred Curtis at last made up his mind to resign his position, and go to England to consult with Father Newman. He returned a Catholic and entered Saint Mary's Seminary to prepare for the priesthood. A year later, John Tabb too had become a Catholic, to the amazement of relatives and friends — in fact, to the utter horror of some of them. The first confession Father Curtis heard as a priest was that of John Tabb, and through the years Tabb and Father Curtis — later Bishop Curtis of Delaware — remained close to each other.

In 1874, John Tabb entered St. Charles College to study for the classical degree. On his graduation he was given the chair of English in the college and he occupied it until his death in 1909. He studied for the priesthood while teaching, but was not ordained until 1884. His friend Cardinal Gibbons had in a single day given him four of the Sacraments — baptism, penance, Holy Communion, and confirmation in old Saint Peter's at Baltimore, and later he also gave him Holy Orders.

Tabb wrote Sidney Lanier about his new faith. They had occasionally visited each other and never ceased writing since the days in the war prison, and often Lanier wished he could see more of John — "especially a walk with this lovely April unearthliness in the atmosphere," he wrote one spring.

But though he had so far shared things with John, to his friend's conversion Lanier was cold. "I long ago outgrew the possibility of such narrowness," he wrote. "But an earnest belief is always beautiful to me." Once later he wrote that he was reading Thomas à Kempis and John's hopes rose. But neither à Kempis nor anything else ever drew Lanier to his friend's faith.

They remained close friends nevertheless, for they had many things in common. For one thing, they were and remained rebels to the end. Father Tabb rarely if ever went north of the Mason and Dixon line. Once invited to visit a friend named Barrett who lived in Nebraska, he declined in verse :

> "Who would think on
> A Rebel in Lincoln ?
> Or venture to ask a
> Friend to Nebraska ?
> Another might dare it —
> But I cannot, Barrett."

When an admiring cleric wrote to him about his verses and compared him with Emerson, Father Tabb retorted that he was a Roman Catholic and a red-hot rebel and he hated Emerson. Perhaps this last was because of the Concord philosopher's defense of Abolition years ago, or perhaps it came from Father Tabb's impatience with the somewhat cloudy messages of Transcendentalism. He did not live to know that in 1916 the Oxford University Press, in its volume called *Epigrams*, included the verse of only two Americans : Emerson — and Tabb. Perhaps it was as well.

The little melody Lanier had played in prison haunted

Tabb until one day he managed to put it down on a page. After that he often played it over to remind him of his absent friend.   As for Lanier, he once said that "Tabb was one of the best and truest souls that ever lived." "All the badness he ever knew I taught him," he added with a smile.

Occasionally Tabb found time to visit the Laniers and it was Lanier who often read and criticized his friend's verses and helped in selecting the best magazines to which to send them, for Tabb had no ideas whatsoever on such matters.   Lanier, himself no mean poetic genius, thought Tabb's "minute, delicately carven work" among the great poetry of America.   His own favorite was :

> "Oh, Shadow in thy fleeting form I see
> The friend of fortune who once clung to me —
> In flattering light thy constancy is shown ;
> In darkness, thou wilt leave me all alone."

Father Tabb loved to visit the Laniers because of the love of music they shared.   "You can't know Beethoven unless you feel his soul beating in the ends of your fingers," Lanier once wrote him, and Tabb agreed with all his heart.

When his college duties were done at St. Charles Father Tabb was wont to visit the recreation room where the piano stood and the chapel where the organ was. He preferred the recreation room at times when there were no students there, but if, after he began playing, a crowd came in, he never noticed them until he had finished.

He enjoyed good singing too, though his own voice was a high odd one. Once when he had admired the voice of a young prima donna, one rather Puritanical critic objected to his praise since her private life was not all it should have been. He shrugged impatiently. "If a nightingale were singing outside my window, I would listen to him no matter how many times he had been divorced," he said.

The one thing he could not bear was ragtime. If he heard it played he walked out, no matter where he was. And the invention of the mechanical piano drove him wild, because of the often faulty timing. "Butchered," he would mutter and go away hastily.

Tabb loved teaching. He was a born teacher, and his special delight was in his Greek and English classes. He taught with a mixture of eagerness, earnestness, and fun, the latter usually consisting of a stream of puns, but there was never in them any bitterness or sting. He wrote a grammar too — *Bone Rules of English Grammar* he called it and he dedicated it to his pupils — "active and passive, past, present and future, perfect and imperfect," and later added in one student's book, "and in whatever mood they may be."

He made his students, if not love, at least appreciate, literature. Once, when he called on a young man to ask him a question about the "Ode to a Nightingale" and saw no response in his face, he stopped suddenly and stared at him. "Child, have you never read it ?" he asked incredulously. He loved Keats and Poe and Herrick among others. And he loved Emily Dickinson's verse and said it was "poetry pulled up by the roots."

He did not, however, keep only to the poets in his classes. Often the discussion turned on current affairs, for even though some thought him lost in a world of poesy, he always watched public events closely. When the United States annexed the Philippines, he wrote a sympathetic quatrain to the Filipinos :

> "We 've come to give you liberty,
>   To do whate'er we choose ;
>   Or clear extermination,
>   If you venture to refuse."

Such verse he called "a sneeze" and he wrote a great deal of it, much of it filled with his insatiable love of making puns. Once, when Bishop Foley of Michigan was visiting Cardinal Gibbons the two were invited to dinner at the College and Tabb was delegated to write the invitation. The prelate was no doubt astonished when he opened the note and read :

> "Dear Cardinal Gibbons,
>   With all your red ribbons,
>   Pray lend us the light of your face —
>   And bring with you Holy
>   John Michigan Foley,
>   (Who hopes some day to be in your place.)"

He punned even on the affliction of blindness which overtook him in later years. "This blindness," he said, "is not as black as it 's painted." And Bishop Curtis told how Tabb at a time when his sight was threatened, and when he asked if there were any message he could take from Tabb to Cardinal Gibbons, answered, "Oh, yes — ask him to give me a new See."

For years poetry poured from Tabb's pen — child verse, quatrains, puns, nature verse, poems of faith.   "With a sunset, a rainbow, and a pun John Tabb was a happy man," someone said of him.

His fame as a poet grew rather slowly.   His first book of verse, published in 1884, was privately printed, and during the next ten years his poems appeared only in magazines.   When, in 1894, his second volume was published it ran through four printings in a single year. His simple, natural quatrains, his homely homemade way of putting deep truths won him many readers.

Critics began to compare him with noted writers — Blake, Poe, Francis Thompson — "only without his moodiness."   And Alice Meynell in 1907 made a selection of his verse for a volume, which he in turn dedicated to her.   *The Athenaeum* said he was a rare discovery, something like Shelley with a bit of Poe, a lyric poet whose verse was in the romantic style but who was a realist in the world's true sense.   And *The New Century* called him one of the most vital forces in contemporary letters and said, "He carries the credentials of genius."   Edmund Stedman spoke of his "flawless lyrics," and *The London Times* of his verse's grandeur.   "A lapidary among song makers," someone called him, and another "a man who sees the spiritual in the natural."

Not all of them caught the one reason for the vitality

of his verse — that it was informed with a passionate love
of the dogmas of the Church.   "The very arrangement
of the liturgical year," says M. S. Pine, one of his biogra-
phers, "is a suggested epic, based as it is on the deep par-
allel between the evolution of the seasons and that of the
Christian soul of the human race."   Tabb never made
the error of so many of his day ; he never confused the
purely natural with the supernatural.   "He counted the
stars," said George Shuster, "but his eye shot past them
to the Hand of Love that had stitched the embroidery."

His deep love of Our Lady is found in many a poem and
it is summed up in one especially :

> "Nor Bethlehem, nor Nazareth
> Apart from Mary's care ;
> Nor Heaven itself a home for Him
> Were not His Mother there."

Even in much of his children's verse there is often a re-
flection of the manger at Bethlehem :

> "Goodnight, dear Lord !  and now
> Let them that loved to keep
> Thy little bed in Bethlehem
> Be near me while I sleep ;
> For I — more helpless, Lord — of them
> Have greater need than Thou."

Essentially joyous in his faith, even in his poems on
Gethsemane, there is always the light of an Easter soon
to come.   And what never escaped him was the fact of
the smallness of man and the greatness of his Creator.

He had a great dignity about him but he was so friendly

and so simple a man that for all his erudition no one ever thought of him as the Reverend John Bannister Tabb, M. A. ; he was Father Tabb to everyone. He remained, as he had been a homely baby, a homely man, very tall, with prominent features, and extremely thin — "wholly released from the flesh" he used to say.

Though he was a sociable being among those he knew well, he fled from strangers like a wild thing. He hated people in a crowd and on the eve of the Feast of Saint Charles he went miles away from the college so that he might avoid the swarm of visitors. He did not like farewells either : no one ever saw him leave the college for his summer vacations to his old home. Before commencement was well begun his room was empty : the bird had flown.

He had never complained about the loss of friends and loss of companionship which his conversion to Catholicism had brought him. But it must have been very hard for him to leave the known and come to live as he did among strangers. His humility was great. After his ordination as deacon he was with difficulty persuaded to go higher. He planned to remain a deacon and keep on teaching. But his superiors insisted he be ordained priest and he gave in.

Holy Orders were conferred on him during Advent, and the midnight Mass of Christmas was his first Mass. He was so deeply affected by the greatness and the sacredness of the act that he would celebrate only one instead of the permitted three. Afterward he gave a short sermon, mostly as thanks to his students for the beautiful chalice which he had just used and which they had given him. His chief desire, he told them, was that he might spend his life working with his students and offer the sacrifice of the Mass for the last time in this chapel where he had just offered it for the first time. That prayer was answered. He said Mass there always, save during the holidays when he was away. And he taught there all his years.

Daily before school began he said Mass. But his meditations began even earlier and were very long. Once his server came at four by mistake instead of at five and found Father Tabb already there, kneeling in prayer. And at any time during day or night the tall gaunt form, the slender hands lovingly clasped about a book of prayer, might have been seen in the gallery chapel.

Toward the end of his life he celebrated Mass more and more from memory, for the eyes that had never been strong grew suddenly weaker. By 1908 his sight was so dim that he needed strong magnifying glasses to read a letter and usually had to dictate the answers. But he needed no eyes to see the spiritual world, and happy events of the past remained in his heart. He wrote :

> "The tenderness of visions gone
> In shadow seems to stay."

His server was always at hand to prompt him, but, during the last years of his life, when he was practically blind, he never faltered once. He taught no more during those years, but he refused a pension, saying he would pay full board as long as he could.   And he was never lonely even when alone, for he had three loves left him ; his music, his verse, and his faith.

The year before his death he spent many hours in the college chapel at the organ, and he still wrote much verse. Despite his blindness his poetry retained its customary cheerfulness ; only here and there is a poem which shows his pain.   A verse in the *Atlantic Monthly* showed how he wrought his blindness into the fabric of his spiritual life as he had all the other happenings.   He was learning in the School of Darkness

> "What mean
> The Things unseen."

And another poem ended :

> "Amid falling rain
> Of tears, I lift, O Lord, mine eyes to Thee,
> For lo, I *see*."

By the fall of 1909 he was very feeble.   He died on November 19th of that year and lay in state at Saint Charles College, his students forming a guard of honor about him.   His funeral Mass was sung on a gray day of mist and rain.   The church was filled with his students — "past and present" — with priests and professors, friends of his long life, and with Confederate veterans who had known him long ago and never forgotten him. The governor of the state was an honorary pall bearer.

He was buried in Hollywood Cemetery at Richmond.

One of his own quatrains would have served him well as epitaph :

"IN AETERNUM

If Life and Death be things that seem,
If Death be sleep and Life a dream,
May not the everlasting sleep
The dream of Life Eternal keep ?"

# LUCY SMITH

## MOTHER CATHERINE DE RICCI
## [1845–1894]

*"To give to others the fruit
of contemplation."*

The Dominican Order has two mottoes, "To praise, to bless, to teach," and "To give to others the fruit of contemplation." This is the story of a woman who practised in her life the fusion of those two beliefs of Saint Dominic.

When William Smith, a well known engineer of the City of New York, named the third child of his family of seven Lucy, he could not see that years later she was to bear a very different name — Mother Catherine de Ricci of the Sacred Heart of Christ.

Lucy Eaton Smith's family moved from Brooklyn into New York City in the early 1850's, when Lucy was still a small girl, and bought a big house on West Twenty-third Street. She went to the fashionable boarding day school of Madame Mears on Fifteenth Street, and enjoyed her life at school as much as she did her happy family life at home.

There was little of religion mentioned or practised in the Smith household. Mr. Smith was only nominally a Presbyterian and Mrs. Smith read much of the humanist literature of the day and proclaimed herself a deist. It was, then, the grandmother, Mrs. McIntyre, a devout Episcopalian, who gave the children what religion they had in their lives, and it was she who saw to it that Lucy was confirmed in that denomination at the age of fourteen.

The Catholic Faith draws its chosen in many and varied ways. For Lucy the path led at first through music. She was appreciative of that art rather than herself talented, and she spent many happy hours in the big parlor at home, sitting quietly in a corner listening to her sister Mary and Mary's friend, Adelina Patti, singing duets together. She admired her sister's voice with intense family loyalty but she had to admit to herself that Adelina's voice was better than Mary's.

Her own room was on the side of the house that faced the French Church of Saint Vincent de Paul. On Sundays she used to sit close to her window and listen to the singing of High Mass next door. After a while she decided she wanted to see as well as to hear, and one Sunday she slipped in with the crowds and spent a wonderful hour listening to the chanting and feasting her eyes on candles and blue clouds of incense and soft colored vestments.

Sunday after Sunday she went there, understanding nothing of the ceremonies at all, but loving it and feeling content just to be a part of it. When, on a week day as she was starting out for school unusually early, she saw people going into the church, she followed them and was surprised to find the Sunday ceremonies were being repeated. Only the music was missing on a week day.

When the service was over — she had forgotten all about school — she went shyly up to the altar for the first time, and knelt for long minutes at the rail, not praying, not even thinking, just loving it all, looking at it all.

One of her playmates who was a Catholic saw her as she came out of the church. "Are you a Catholic?" she asked in surprise.

Lucy shook her head. "Oh, no."

"Then why are you kneeling in our church and adoring the Blessed Sacrament?" demanded the other girl.

Lucy stared at her. "Adore the Blessed Sacrament," she replied. "But I don't even know what that is. I never heard of it. I just went there and knelt because I wanted to and because I really couldn't help myself."

Interested in such religious zeal, her friend took her one day to see Father Alfred Young of the Paulist Fathers, to whom she had told the strange story of the little girl who knelt in a Catholic church and didn't know why. Gradually, Lucy Smith learned why she was kneeling at that altar. And gradually she learned about the Faith from Father Young who had seldom had a more interested pupil or one who so quickly saw the essentials of the Faith. She was not quite twenty-one when she was conditionally baptized in the church of Saint Paul the Apostle. As she knelt before him, her innocent face lifted, her eyes shining, Father Young thought that the snow falling outside the church seemed an emblem of the purity of this girl.

When her family learned how deep had become Lucy's devotion to the Catholic Church there was deep perturbation. At first they had all been amused at her devotion, but they had not expected her to take it as seriously as this.

To attend Catholic services was a vagary of no importance, but when they learned that she actually wanted to become a Catholic there were objections.

Mrs. Smith loved society and the social New York of that day had not much use for Catholics.   In fact, Mrs. Smith was afraid it might upset her own social status if it were known that her daughter had allied herself with the Catholic Church.

Her brothers and sisters teased Lucy mightily about it — all but Lillie.   Lillie was twelve and adored her big sister and admired everything she did.   As for Mr. Smith, his objections did not last long.   In fact he seemed to be impressed with his daughter's daring and her sincerity and often he went with her to High Mass.   Later he held a pew in his own name at Saint Vincent's.

When Lucy was twenty-two years old her father died suddenly.   Her grief was deepened by the fact that he had never actually become a Catholic, and she had hoped for his eventual conversion, since he had evinced so great a friendliness for the Faith.

The family was completely broken up now, as several of the children had already married and gone to homes of their own and some were living in other cities.   For a time only Mrs. Smith and Lucy and Lillie formed the family circle, and at Lucy's insistence her mother sent Lillie to school at the Visitation Convent at Riverdale. And, at her mother's insistence, though rather against her own will, Lucy and her mother went to live in a boarding house — a very fashionable one which Mrs. Smith found much to her liking.

By this time Lucy herself was unhappily certain that she must soon get entirely away from her family for a time in order to decide on her vocation in life. Knowing that Lillie was in excellent hands and that her mother was in the very place where she most wanted to be and would not need her, she used her poor health as an excuse to go on a vacation to Europe. It was in Germany, in Berlin, that she found the man who understood what she was trying to do, a thing she herself hardly understood. She put herself under the spiritual guidance of Father Aquilanti, Prior of the Dominican Convent there, and followed his advice from that time on.

"I am afraid your health is not equal to a regular religious life," he told her.

She nodded sadly. "I am afraid of that too. Perhaps, I sometimes say to myself, my entire vocation is to convert my own family."

He smiled at her and shook his head. "I think there will be something more. Meantime wait and pray."

Lucy spent three years in Europe, visiting shrines and convents everywhere — Fourvière, Ouillins, Annecy, where she implored Saint Francis de Sales to help point out her way to her.

During her third year abroad, she heard that Father Aquilanti had been exiled by Bismarck and was now Prior of Santa Sabina in Rome. She went to see him immediately and found him happy in his new home — for was this not the place where Thomas of Aquin and Vincent Ferrer had both lived and prayed and worked ?

Father Aquilanti felt that Lucy was now ready for some definite plan of her life.   Her health had improved, and her knowledge of things Catholic had greatly increased during her years abroad.   They decided that she would become a secular Dominican tertiary.   For the years had at least made one thing clear to her : she must realize the vision of which she had so far had only a glimpse — to live a life in Christ.

Father Aquilanti told her he felt it was time now for her to go back to her own land.   "But not," he added, "to the Cenacle Sisters or to the Dominicans either.   I feel you are ready now to make a foundation for the purposes you have so often mentioned to me."

"Perhaps I should stay a while in England or France among the Dominicans," she suggested.

"No, your own bustling America needs you," he said, "and for just the work you propose.   You need no novitiate either, for you have had your novitiate in the world."

They discussed the work she hoped to do — something to further retreats, something to open up to many women who were of the laity the way of life that had done so much for her.   She visioned an order of nuns to whom women could go, women whose lives had not perhaps sufficient religious vitality and who did not know how to go about it for themselves, nuns who knew the world and its problems, whose time was taken up entirely with edu-

cational or hospital work.    This sort of nun was needed,
Father Aquilanti and she both felt, for the sort of group
she hoped to establish.    He sped her on her way with his
blessing.

One happy bit of news she took home with her — at
least happy to her.    Her sister Isabella, married and living in Europe, had become a Catholic.    Her mother received the news with no joy.

"So now that is good news," she said sarcastically.    "I
suppose now the two of you can be nuns and found a
convent."    And she looked with disfavor, too, at the
simple black dress that Lucy was wearing — her pretty
Lucy who ought to have a gay life in Mrs. Smith's own
social world.

She tried with all her persuasiveness to lure Lucy back
into society, and Lucy yielded when she could, for her
adopted rule, she knew, must never stand in the way of
charity.    And one day Lucy came home to find her
mother in tears.    Lillie was there, in tears too, and Lucy
looked bewildered from one to the other.

"Lucy," her mother wailed, "it is all your fault.    Now
here is Lillie saying that she is going to be a Catholic too.
Just wait until your grandmother hears about this."

Grandmother heard about it and was as vexed as Mrs.
Smith had said she would be.    "She is furious and won't
talk to me at all," Lucy confided to a friend, "but how can
I feel badly about it when it means that my Lillie is in
the Church at last, as I always hoped she would be.    That
makes three of us now."

Father Aquilanti's scheme, Lucy soon learned, was no simple matter to impress upon the clergy with whom she discussed it. The Dominican Provincial to whom Father Aquilanti had suggested she go felt the only place for active nuns was in schools and hospitals. But he thought highly of Father Aquilanti himself and he liked the fervor with which Lucy put forward her ideas.

"I know two convert Sisters — Dominican tertiaries like yourself. Why don't the three of you make a foundation and for a beginning take care of orphans? Then later on retreats can be the work of some of the Sisters as your group grows and the rest of you can stay with the orphans."

Lucy agreed, since it seemed the best she could hope for for the time being. She joined the other two women and together they began their work in a little house on Second Avenue in New York City. Now, for the first time and because she was a professed Dominican tertiary, she put on the white habit of her Order and took a name in religion. She chose that of Catherine de Ricci, a Dominican mystic and stigmatist of whom she had read a great deal while she was in Europe, and who especially appealed to her because of her devotion to the Blessed Sacrament.

It was not her fault that this first attempt ended in failure. Two brief months showed her that the work among the orphans was not for her, and that for what she wished to do there was but little chance for a long time. She went home again and devoted the next two years mainly to studying the life of the Ursuline and

Visitation orders. Several times she went to Cardinal McCloskey with her cherished hope, but he was very hesitant about granting permission, not entirely because he disapproved of the idea, for he was quite in favor of it, but because there were no funds available in the diocese to make such a foundation practicable, and Lucy's small income was insufficient.

She spent a time quietly with her mother and grandmother in the latter's home on Staten Island, busying herself with instructing the parish children and preparing them for the Sacraments. She started religious study groups and formed sewing clubs.

But she never forgot what she wanted to accomplish. And one day, when she was visiting at Glen Falls, she saw an empty building near the church where she had just heard Mass. Suddenly the thought came to her that here was a place where she might begin her work and unite it with the sort of work she had been doing at Staten Island.

She went to the pastor and told him of her desire and promised she would do parish teaching in order to get the other work started. To her joy she found that he looked on this suggestion as an inspiration from the Holy Spirit and immediately made arrangements with the Bishop of Albany to make a foundation there.

This time Lucy Smith made her vows for three years as a conventual Dominican tertiary and the two companions who had been with her before rejoined her. They had, of course, to maintain a school, for that was part of the bargain.

Once more her hopes were blighted, for the house proved so unhealthy that the postulants who came went away again almost as fast as they came. The tiny community could find no other house suited to them near the church, so they moved to West Troy, where again they tried to popularize retreats and where they were again made welcome by the priests who again insisted that they conduct a free school in addition to the retreat work.

Mother de Ricci thought it was time to take a bold step, or the rest of her life would be passed in this unsatisfactory way and the work she felt she should be doing would never get done. So partly with her own small funds, and by placing mortgages on the property, a house was bought on the Albany-Troy post road; a formal novitiate was established and, with no provisos about schools or any other parochial work, retreats for lay women were announced.

The small community was amazed at the response. The success of the project was immediate. Women came from New York and Boston, even from as far away as Washington, as well as groups from around Troy itself, to attend the offered retreats.

Within two years Lucy Smith's hope had become a full reality. At the Bishop's suggestion the community now moved to Albany and there rented a house and set about the purchasing of a new permanent dwelling for a mother-house. And, when that was bought Mother de Ricci brought for the chapel altar the relic of Catherine de Ricci, which had been given her by the Dominican nuns at Florence.

Now that she had a small corps of responsible women working with her, she decided to take a quick trip abroad to ask the Master General of the Dominicans for affiliation with the Order.   He proved very amenable and helpful, and arranged that she assist at the Pope's Mass and receive Communion from the Holy Father himself.   He also arranged for her an audience and the Pope, learning that she was a Dominican, gave her a special blessing, his hand on her head.

She hurried home.   The Sisters were in their new house now and she was eager to be a part of it.   A regular conventual routine was established.   The Blessed Sacrament, her source of grace even before she came into the Church, her strength and consolation ever since, naturally was the chief devotion of the Community.   It made her sad to see people seeking something to love and someone to love, when "if they turned to the Blessed Sacrament they would find the perfection of love."   She managed to have Exposition in her chapel as often as possible, feeling it was the best way to change people's hearts and give them strength.

The active work of the Sisters was now just what Lucy Smith had always wanted it to be : assisting the chaplain to give retreats to women who came to stay at the convent for a few days for this special purpose, the conducting of catechism classes for adults as well as for children, Bible and study classes, the making of vestments and maintaining a guest house for women who wished to live in that quiet convent atmosphere, the fostering of days of recollection.

In March, Mother de Ricci made her perpetual vows and in November she received the long desired diploma of aggregation to the Dominican Order. It seemed the very time to begin a new foundation ; so one was opened at Saratoga Springs. But the old Lucy Smith luck of difficult beginnings was operating again. The Sisters met with violent opposition from the priest there ; he opposed their work so vehemently that when they appeared at Mass he denounced them and all their "idle life," and the Bishop finally had to dispense them from Sunday Mass on days when they had no chaplain at their house. But other priests were more friendly and the work finally began to operate successfully.

Perhaps it was that she had worked too hard, and perhaps it was that her health had never been enough for her efforts. Whatever the reason, she was less than fifty years old when she died, just fourteen years after she had established the foundation at Saratoga Springs. But her work had proved groundless that early fear of hers that her entire vocation was only to convert her own family.

At that, she had done very well with her family. In the early days Lillie had been of great help in sending supplies and with her constant prayers. In 1888 she had the joy of giving the postulant's cap to this especially loved sister. Five years earlier her sister Isabella, home from Europe a widow, had entered the Community.

"Now I have someone for ballast," Lucy had rejoiced when she heard that news. Grandmother McIntyre, who had been so enraged when Lucy became a Catholic, finally accepted an invitation to visit at the retreat house. The visit lasted over five years and ended in Grandmother McIntyre, at the age of ninety-four, coming into the Church. In 1890 her mother was received and the next year her brother, John. Her grandmother, her mother, all her sisters and brothers save one — it was a good record and perhaps would have been enough for one person to accomplish for the Faith. But the record has gone much further. She had, in her retreats, brought many closer to the Faith or actually into the Church. She had made many strong again in their Faith who had grown weak.

Lucy Smith had held firmly to her one purpose, yielding over and over only so that later she might push on again. The result has been not only the motherhouse in Albany, the house at Saratoga Springs, but a retreat house and a home for working girls in Philadelphia, foundations in New York City, in Dayton, a great retreat house in Elkins Park, and, at the request of the Bishop of Cuba, foundations there to care for Spanish war orphans to do spiritual work among the Cuban women and the building of two academies where English is taught.

"Don't trouble yourself about too many things," Lucy Smith had once said to her sister Lillie, "if we understand all, where would be our trust?" And the motto of her Congregation well exemplified the aim of her life : "Pati et contemni per Te."

# ROSE HAWTHORNE LATHROP

## MOTHER ALPHONSA

[1851–1926]

*"Human beings owe a debt
of love to one another."*

The inheritance which a father bequeathes to his daughter is not always merely money or houses or stocks. It is sometimes a mental, social, or spiritual inheritance.

To his youngest daughter, whom he affectionately called the Rose of all the Hawthornes, Nathaniel Hawthorne left various legacies. He left her the memory of a brave gentleman, a sensitive soul ; he left her the memory of happy days spent with him in Italy — in Rome, where the seeds of faith were sown in her that later ripened to fruition. But, best of all, he left her his love of humankind, even the most wretched — and a sense of duty towards them, a feeling of service that must be rendered mentally or physically, with the pen or the voice or perhaps with the devotion of a lifetime.

Rose was a very small child when her father was appointed American consul at Liverpool. In England he was made much of, invited to great houses, hunted, as she put it in the charming book she wrote about him many years later, "to gorgeous dinners against his better instincts." For the Hawthornes never cared much for gorgeousness — unless it were that of a sunset or a great deed. In one of her letters to her father in the United

States, Mrs. Hawthorne wrote of the "hideous condition of the very poor — this most crying and worst of evils." That was the sort of thing the Hawthornes were most likely to notice.

Along with the grandeur of the stately homes to which Hawthorne was being continually invited, he saw also the terrible squalor and poverty of England's poor. One morning of a dark English February in 1856 he went with several friends to visit the West Derby workhouse. He was shown through the different rooms, and the bare poverty, the coldness of charity, and what he called the "atmosphere of the house of paupers" filled him with dismay.

To a woman walking beside him he said, "It is a curious thing — this atmosphere. For no matter how fastidiously we breathe it in we are forced to inhale it into our inmost being. If even the Queen were here, I know not how she would escape the necessity." The woman who walked beside him looked in surprise at him as if she thought this American a bit odd.

Later in his notebooks Hawthorne recorded the incident which occurred on this visit to the workhouse and which so mightily moved him. "What an intimate brotherhood is this in which we dwell, do what we may to put an artificial remoteness between the high creature and the low. It is but an example of how by every moment in our lives the flow and reflux of a common humanity pervades us all. How superficial are the niceties of such as pretend to keep aloof. Let the whole world be cleansed or not a man or woman of us can be clean."

He went into the children's ward, as unpleasant and unwholesome as was the rest of the establishment. In a corner where several grimy children were playing together, one detached itself from the group and came over to the visitor — a child of six, its face disfigured with something which the Governor of the workhouse who was their guide said was scurvy. The child came straight to Hawthorne, not even noticing the others, smiled up at him, took hold of his coat, followed him around as they went about the ward and then standing directly in front of him, lifted its arms with the confidence his own little Rose would have shown, and without any words plainly showed it wanted the visitor to pick it up. Hawthorne was a person with a great love of niceties and cleanliness and the soiled little mite below him clutching at his knees made him hesitate a moment, but only for a moment. There was such confidence in the small face that he stooped and gathered the soiled atom in his arms. "It was," he wrote later, "as if God had promised the child this favor in my behalf and I must needs fulfil the contract."

So he held the little thing for a while and, even after he had put it down again, it followed him about, held two of his fingers in its scrawny blotched hand, playing with them — "as if it were a child of my own," he thought. They went into another part of the wards, but after they came down there was the child again with its dim red eyes and the sickly smile on its defaced mouth — "I should never have forgiven myself had I repelled its advances," he told his wife that evening.

Later in the day he was taken to another house — this time a lovely English home, with great sloping lawns and carefully tended gardens. And that evening he wrote in his diary : "I wonder how many people live and die in the workhouse having no other home, because other people have a great deal more home than enough."

When the family left England they went to Rome to live for a time. This city Rose's father learned to love dearly and so did her mother. Here the New England Protestantism in them both grew dim sometimes as the brightness of Catholic realities began to shine before them. They all loved Rome — the parents, serious sixteen-year-old Una, Julian, the sturdy ten-year-old son of the house, and usually Rose the youngest also.

Rose, however, was not so moved by Rome as were the others. Years later she wrote in retrospect of the great impression made on her by the Holy Father on his balcony, but the strangeness of the Latin prayers chanted in the streets made her feel it was all a child's game, and no one explained them to her. During Lent she watched cakes being fried in oil and sold on the streets and tasted them. She wrote, "I found them to be indistinct in taste for all their pretty tint and the dexterous twist of the cook's wrist as he picked them up. If they had been appetizing I should have been sharply interested in the idea of becoming a Catholic, but their entire absence of relish convinced me that the Italians lacked mental grasp and salvation at a single swoop."

It was not until she was grown up and a Catholic herself that she realized how close both her parents had come to the Faith during their years in Rome. "They didn't believe that Italy was really under an incubus, and they felt the spiritual weight of Catholicism and of the Cross and half guessed its spiritual meaning."

Mrs. Hawthorne wrote home to her family about a visit to Saint Peter's. "There alone in Rome is perpetual summer. It would seem warmed by the ardent soul of Peter, or the breath of prayer from innumerable saints." Then, too, her dear friend, Anna Ward, had been recently received into the Church. Though both Nathaniel Hawthorne and his wife had Catholic spirits, they remained, so far as their outer faith went, purely Protestant. Yet Hawthorne could write about the Eternal City that "the desolation of its ruins does not prevent her from being more intimately our home than even the spot where we were born." And that spot was Puritan New England !

The Hawthornes went back home to their little house in Concord, with its pleasant outlook on the Lexington Road. And, after a few happy years there, Hawthorne died and was buried with Concord men in Sleepy Hollow burial ground. The rest of the family went to live in Europe and while in England Mrs. Hawthorne died. Una decided to stay there and to become a member of an Anglican sisterhood. Julian and Rose came home and not long after George Parsons Lathrop, whom they had met abroad, joined them and persuaded Rose to be his wife.

Then came news of the sudden death of Una in London,

and Rose scarcely realized this loss when it was followed
by another — that of her four-year-old son Francis, the
Lathrops' only child.   Shortly after this Rose and her
husband were received into the Catholic Faith in the
Paulist Church in New York City.

Of all her family only Julian was left now, and her
husband.   But though she had striven with all her heart
to make her married life a success she was not able to do
so.   It was not that she did not love George Lathrop, for
she did and dearly.   But there were inherent weaknesses
in him and an instability that finally forced her to leave
him.   She went back to him several times, until at last
she saw there was no use in trying again.

Now her life was very empty.   One day in an effort to
forget her troubles, she decided to look up a dressmaker
who used to work for her, and have some gowns made
over.   She learned that the woman had been a victim of
cancer and had been taken to the City Home on Black-
well's Island.   She went to see her and found she had
died and been buried before she reached the Island.   But
during her brief visit there she had seen the horror of what
it meant to be one of the cancerous poor, shunted off to
the City Home to die.   A dear friend of hers, Emma
Lazarus, had recently died of that disease and she had
seen how much her friend had suffered, even though surrounded by every comfort and care.   It seemed a terrible
thing, she mused on her way home, to endure such pain
and receive no comfort, no tending, merely because one
was poor.   Worst of all, at that time cancer was thought

to be contagious and often the family itself drew away from the sufferer.

She came home to her empty rooms, sick at heart. Her own sadness was forgotten in the thought of the misery she had seen. She sat down and drew from her bookshelves one of her father's books, as she often did. To-night especially she felt she must be a little in touch with someone who had loved her.

The volume she picked up was "Our Old Home," the sketches of his year in England and she read over paragraphs of his life there. She had herself been too young to remember much of it, but even so some of those days came back to her.

She turned the pages and her eye fell on his account of his visit to the workhouse — the diseased child who followed him — how he felt he was responsible for it and dared not let it go without comforting it. He wrote in the third person, as he often did about himself. "No doubt the child's mission was to remind him that he was responsible in his degree for all the sufferings and mis-demeanors of the world in which he lived, and was not entitled to look upon a particle of its dark calamity as if it were none of his concern : the offspring of a brother's iniquity being his own blood-relation, and the guilt, like-wise, a burden on him, unless he expiated it by better deeds. It might almost make a man doubt the existence of his own soul, to observe how nature has flung the little wretches into the street and left them there, so evidently regarding them as nothing worth, and how all mankind acquiesces in the great mother's estimate of her offspring. For if they have no immortality, what superior claims can I assert for mine ? And how difficult to believe that anything so precious as a gem of immortal growth can have been buried under this dirt heap, plunged in this cesspool of misery and vice. Ah, what a mystery. Slowly, slowly, as after groping at the bottom of a deep, noisome, stagnant pool, my hope struggles upward to the surface, bearing the half drowned body of a child along with it and heaving it aloft for its life and my life and all our lives. Unless these slime-clogged nostrils can be made capable of inhaling celestial air, I know not how the purest and most intellectual of us can reasonably expect to taste a breath of it. The whole question of eternity is staked here. If a single one of these helpless ones is lost, the world is lost."

It seemed to her that she was learning a lesson just as her father had taught her years ago. She turned to another page. "Human beings owe a debt of love to one another," he had written, "because there is no other method of paying the debt of love and care which all of us owe Providence which put me here among other things, in order that I may make amends for the inhospitality of my neighbors."

She knew now that there was something for her to do. The first thing was to take away, as much as was in her power, the look of horror and fear she had seen on the faces in the cancer ward at the Island. She enrolled for a course in cancer nursing, and found she had indeed embarked on a hard work. When the nursing was finished, she rented, with money contributed by friends, a small two-room flat in lower New York and announced it would be a free home for incurable cancer patients. There would be only two rules to govern the venture : patients must be entirely without funds and there must be no hope of any cure. At first she could take only one or two women patients in the house itself, and the rest of the work was among patients who came to have their sores dressed.

When the *Times* learned that Mrs. George Parsons Lathrop, a member of New York's best social group, a woman who had books to her credit, whose father had been one of America's great geniuses, was devoting herself to work among the slum's cancerous outcasts, the paper sent a reporter to get details of such a remarkable story. When the people who had met her at parties and the opera read this they could not believe their eyes.

Not long afterwards the *Times* chronicled in a paragraph the death of G. P. Lathrop and stated, "Mrs. Lathrop was at his bedside when he died."

Her name through the years was often in the *Times* in the letters she wrote appealing for help for her work — letters that had literary value as well as heart value, for had Rose Lathrop chosen to follow a literary path, there is no doubt she would have become one of our remembered writers.

From here and there the money came — never much, but enough to keep the work going. The patients, hear-

ing of this chance for help without having to go to the
dreaded Island, came in numbers to the little flat and
Mrs. Lathrop treated them as clinic patients.    Only the
worst and saddest she kept in her small space and cared
for them day and night.    When she was able to add two
more rooms to her clinic she was a happy woman.

In the crowded little rooms she kept pain at bay and
brought into the sad lives which entrusted themselves to
her care as much respite from agony as she could and a
certain hope that though this life was ebbing there was
another, with pain no longer even a memory, near at hand
for them.    She had in her two qualities that bore her
through the hardest times : love of God and a deep sense
of joy.

She lived long enough to see the realization of her
fondest wishes and unceasing prayers.    The two poor
little rooms in which she began her work grew into a big
house on Cherry Street, still in use today as one of New
York's best cancer hospitals.    A great group of houses
was built in Westchester to shelter her poor patients ; her
work and her group of workers became a part of the great
Dominican Order, under the patronage of St. Rose of
Lima.

She had chosen in religion the name 'Alphonsa,' after
the saint who had been so devoted to charity for the sick
poor.    She lived up to that name every day.

She lived to be nearly seventy and she never ceased
being busy.    On the day before she died she wrote a
great pile of letters asking for help with the big new

house just built, and laid them at the feet of St. Joseph
in the chapel.   Next morning they found she had died in
her sleep during the night.   It was obvious too that St.
Joseph had indeed helped her, for not one of those letters went unanswered, and the answers were checks and
money.

The spirit of Rose Hawthorne lives on in her homes.
There is in them a sense of gaiety and joy that is not often
seen in institutions of this tragic kind, houses where death
is always as close as the next bed.   Out of tragedy and
sorrow, out of loss and death in her own heart and home,
she had built beauty for God's unfortunates.   When she
was a little girl her mother had showed her God in the
sunrise and the sunset and the small ways of the world,
showed her paintings and statues wrought for love of God.
And her father who had loved his fellow men so much
that he felt the greatest sin was to refuse help to the needy,
showed her how she could help them.   Between them
her parents had given her a love of God and a love of man
and she, an adopted daughter of the Faith, had put this
service into action for Christ's poor.

Nathaniel Hawthorne had indeed given his Rose a
precious inheritance, the realization of personal responsibility, so far as one person can have it, for the pain of the
world.   He was a gentle sensitive man who hated ugliness
and disfigurement but he took the workhouse child in his
arms because it needed his love.   And his daughter, who
also hated the unclean, the hideous — the dainty girl who
shrank from pain and ugliness, the woman who loved

beauty and pleasant living — took that pain and ugliness into her arms as he had taken the disfigured baby.

There is one difference between them.  She held the unclean and the hideously deformed and did not let them go again — at least not until God took them from the safety of her arms to the safety of His own.  Her father had done the philosophizing about it.  He had laid the groundwork for her later life, by his love for his own family and his sympathy and his understanding of the pain of the world.  His great contribution was to help in words ; his books were a plea for pity and understanding for the human soul.  Her contribution, having, as he had not, the power of the Catholic Faith to sustain her, was to transmute her inheritance into deeds, to offer her human sorrow and love and the broken bodies that came to her for helping — to offer them all to God, to unite small human pity to the Everlasting Mercy.

# LEWIS THOMAS WATTSON

Father Paul James Francis
[1863–1938]

*"Ut omnes unum sint."*

Lewis Thomas Wattson was the youngest son of Joseph Newton Wattson, a clergyman of the Protestant Episcopal Church. He was born on January 16, 1863, at Millington, Maryland, where his father had a parish. Soon after his birth the family moved to Kent Island, Maryland, where most of Lewis' childhood and youth were spent.

Mr. Wattson tended toward the ritualistic wing of his church and had once been dismissed from the General Theological Seminary in New York City because of his pro-Roman leanings ; the clergy who controlled the Seminary thought him "a Jesuit in disguise." Later, however, he was ordained, purged of suspicion.

He always inclined toward Catholic teachings and, since he talked freely at home, his young son imbibed some of them. Once, when he was nine, he heard his father tell of a preaching mission he had attended at the Catholic Cathedral in Baltimore. It had been conducted by the Paulist Fathers, he said, and the sermon he heard had greatly impressed him.

"What we need in the Episcopal Church," he told his wife when he came home, "is a preaching order like the Paulists."

Lewis, who admired his father and had a vague idea of some day becoming a minister too, now felt a sudden surge within him.    It was almost as if a voice inside him were saying, "That is what you will some day do — found a preaching order like the Paulists."

Although during his years at college the idea did not come to him again, he did keep to his intention of becoming a minister.    He attended the same seminary where his father had once been accused of being a secret Jesuit, and in 1885 he was ordained and received a call to the rectorship of a church in Kingston, New York.

Throughout his years at the seminary he had been what his father was, a High Churchman of the conservative type.    There were others of that sort in his class, notably Henry Sargent, John McGarvey, and Jesse Albert Locke.    For some years he remained in Kingston, busy with the varied activities of his parish.    But before the seven years he spent there were over, the idea of establishing a preaching order came back into his mind.    By the time he was thirty he felt so keenly this desire, as well as his own calling to such a project, that he was even then considering what name to give this preaching order.    He felt certain that the name should have something to do with the Cross and with Calvary.    He knew it could not be called Holy Cross for there was already an Episcopal order with that name, and other titles he considered had also been pre-empted.

One day, as he was pondering this subject, he remembered how Saint Francis of Assisi had obtained the original rule of the Friars Minor by opening the Gospels in the name of the Trinity. Perhaps, thought Father Watt-son, God might favor him in the same way. So, on Pentecost Sunday of 1893, he knelt before the altar of his church and opened the Bible. There before his eyes lay a verse from Saint Paul's fifth chapter to the Corinthians : "And not only so, but we also joy in God, through Our Lord Jesus Christ, by whom we have now received the Atonement."

Lewis Wattson felt he had his answer. His Society should bear the name of the Atonement. And when, shortly afterward, an offer came to him to become superior of a small group of unmarried clergy who were living the community life in Omaha, Nebraska, and who were known as the Associate Mission, it seemed a providential step for him to take. Perhaps this little group could be made into the first members of the order he wanted to found. He accepted the call and promised to stay with them as superior for three years.

For a time all went well with the Associate Mission under their new superior. The only difficulty, in fact, was Father Wattson's own. The more he read, the more he thought, the more the papal claims seemed real to him. This of course was an idea which most High Churchmen, no matter how advanced they were, did not accept, and it created difficulties for Father Wattson when he aired his views.

During his second year at Omaha he received a letter from a young woman in the East, who really deserves a chapter of her own in this book.   She was Lurana White from Warwick, New York.   Here she had attended the Episcopal school for girls in charge of the Protestant Holy Child Sisters, later herself becoming a member of this order.   As time passed, Sister Lurana, a devoted follower of Saint Francis of Assisi, felt that the Franciscan ideal she loved could not be followed in a community like hers, since the Sisters did not even take vows.   She had heard of Father Wattson and wrote to him of her perplexity, asking if he knew of any Episcopal order for women which was vowed to corporate poverty.

He was forced to tell her there was none, but he wrote that there was a pressing need for such a congregation, and Omaha would be a good place to begin it, for the Bishop there would welcome them.   Sister Lurana accepted, and went ahead with preparations to come, while Father Wattson felt that his cherished desire was on the point of fulfillment : not only would he have preaching friars but sisters of the Atonement as well.

But one day in July, Sister Lurana received a letter that dashed her hopes.   In the midst of her preparation for the new life and her search for young women who would go to Omaha with her, Father Wattson wrote her that he had, after much prayerful study, accepted the papal claims as true, that he would resign from the Associate Mission and that he would probably become a Roman Catholic.   She, however, he added, would still be very welcome there.   But, after Father Wattson's successor at the Mission had outlined what would be their regulations in the matters of ritual and doctrine, Sister Lurana changed her mind about going to Omaha, and decided to stay quietly at home until God's will was made clear to her regarding her future work.

By the end of September 1898, Father Wattson had decided that perhaps there was no reason for abandoning the idea of his Society of the Atonement because he had come to believe in the papal claims. A better idea might be to remain in his communion and pray for the reconciliation of Americans to the Holy See. And the Society could be Franciscan in its rule and aims. Like Sister Lurana, Father Wattson had always had a strong devotion to the Saint of Assisi. The Community was to be named for the Atonement, and Francis had been a Brother of Penance. It was a Franciscan — Father Peto of the Gray Friars — who had once rebuked Henry the Eighth for his sins, and Catherine of Aragon had been a Franciscan tertiary. The English Franciscans, too, had always been loyal to Saint Peter and suffered for him.

When Father Wattson returned to the East he went to see Sister Lurana in her home in Warwick. From that meeting evolved the Society of the Atonement. Sister Lurana had learned of an abandoned chapel close to Garrison-on-the-Hudson. It had fallen into decay and been restored somewhat by some pious Episcopal women who wished to put it in charge of sisters of their communion. It was called Saint John's-in-the-Wilderness and the location it stood on was known as Graymoor.

Father Wattson visited the place and thought it an ideal location for the Society.   Sister Lurana made ready to go there and begin her foundation.   A single companion went with her, and an old farmhouse was allotted them for their home.   She was among strangers, and she would have to beg for the little she needed to exist on, but she was undaunted.   She had a chapel and she had, she felt certain, the aid of God in her mission.

Not until the following autumn could Father Wattson get his own affairs in the world sufficiently settled to begin his own work.   It was a chill October day in 1899, when he came to the mountainside to decide where to begin.   He had not the money to erect even a small building, but he did have a mountain where apparently no one cared to settle and which, at least for the time being, was his alone.   He saw one bit of a building, apparently an old chicken coop, in too bad shape for anyone to use at the time, but he thought that later it might be put in shape to house, if not himself, some other wanderers who might come there for shelter.

At the foot of the hill he took a knife from his pocket and cut two branches from a fragrant young cedar. With these he fashioned a rude cross, put it on his back and continued on his way up his mountain.   Close to the top he stopped and turned around, and for the first time realized what a task he had set himself.   All about and on each side of him was a wilderness of trees, with hardly a clearing even for the old shed which stood below him.

He was very cold now, for the October wind over the Hudson was a keen one, and he thought perhaps he could find a cave to shelter him better than the dilapidated shed.   But first of all he lifted the cedar cross and planted it firmly on the hilltop.

Despite his search he found no cave, but the farmer who was his nearest neighbor and who had come out to see what this wanderer was doing, offered him a little paint shack on his own property where he might stay for the time being.   He accepted with thanks and spent the winter there, living an ascetic Franciscan life, but with none of the sun of Tuscany to warm him.

He did have an umbrella to protect him from the rain, and often he said his midnight Office with it over him to shield him from the downpour which fell impartially inside and outside the shed.   When the weather was fair enough, he pulled out the old typewriter he had brought with him and began working on the first copy of the magazine he planned to publish to raise funds for building — as soon as he raised funds to publish the magazine !

He sometimes journeyed to New York or to the neighboring parishes where his ritualistic leanings opened doors to him, and he spoke of his hopes of a Franciscan order to be established on his mountainside.   He was a very persuasive speaker and an excellent preacher, so for a time he received donations and gifts, sufficient indeed to begin his magazine and also enough to allow him to build the following year a simple Friary on the mountain. Vocations abounded for him and also for Sister Lurana, and their hopes for an Episcopal Order of Saint Francis were excellent. Sister Lurana kept her own name, but Father Wattson had renamed himself, giving himself in religion the names of three saints to whom he had an especial devotion — Father Paul James Francis.

Suddenly the picture changed. It was of course Father Paul's own fault, for many of the High Church clergy and the laity as well liked his enterprise. He had been greatly in demand for the preaching of missions, but even the most Romeward members of the High Church people were beginning to get nervous at the views he was now expressing. For Father Paul was preaching, with stronger and stronger insistence, the necessity of a return to Rome on the part of the whole Episcopal Church. *The Lamp*, the magazine he had begun in his paint shed, continued the campaign. There were, of course, some who stood firmly with him, but there were many more who objected strongly to hearing a minister of their church declare publicly that Rome must be the center of a reunited Christendom. Before long almost every pulpit of his communion was closed to the Graymoor monk.

Father Paul and the few with him simply retired into their Friary with its small chapel, its office and its seven tiny cells, and from there sent out the issues of *The Lamp*, one after the other. This little magazine had the added value of bringing the Society into close touch with those forces not only in America but also in England, which were working for reunion with Rome. Before long, it spoke out so clearly and so definitely that it became the organ of the pro-Roman party.

The motto of *The Lamp* was "Ut omnes unum sint." As its insignia it pictured a lamp with two flames. It called itself "an Anglo-Catholic Monthly devoted to Church unity"; its cost was one dollar a year. It was an extremely well printed periodical, completely unafraid to voice its opinions, even when it spoke against High Church sympathizers. When *The Living Church*, a leading champion of Anglo-Catholicism, spoke favorably of seeing its communion send bishops — "intruding bishops," said *The Lamp* acidly — to countries where the Catholic Faith was the leading and established faith, such as Mexico, Brazil, and Cuba, *The Lamp* called its arguments specious.

By 1905 the contributors were such outstanding men as Father Vincent McNabb of the Dominicans and Reverend Spencer Jones, both noted English writers. There were articles such as "Infallibility Explained," and "No Creature so near God as Mary." There were extracts from the *Sacred Heart Messenger* and *Ave Maria* and *The Catholic World*, as well as from *The Living Church*.

In 1905 Father Paul asked his readers to pray for the reunion of Christendom, for the Society of the Atonement, for the Society of Saint Thomas of Canterbury (a students' organization) for the Union That Nothing Be Lost — but above all for the restoration of the same relationship between the Anglican Church and the Holy

See that existed before the schism made by Henry the Eighth. "To witness for this as the sine qua non of Church unity in the West is the primary position of *The Lamp*."

The Society of the Atonement made its position very clear, both as to Anglicanism and Roman Catholicism. As for the first, it said it would make no attempt to justify Anglicanism as a system distinct from Peter's Fold. "Since the sixteenth century the Church of England has been a prodigal daughter in her father's house," said one editorial; and another, "The Catholic Revival which in its initial stages produced a Newman, a Manning, and a Faber will in the end produce a whole church purged of Protestant error and rebellion, ripe for Corporate Reunion with the Holy See."

*The Lamp* was very direct in saying it did not care for the idea of effecting union first with the Russian Church. It quoted approvingly what one member of that church once said to Anglican overtures : "First be reconciled to your own Patriarch — then come and talk to us."

From the Episcopalians came continued complaints at this impertinence — and worse. Many felt it was all right to talk reunion, but it was ridiculous to lean to the side of Rome, for it made the movement a laughing stock to both sides. To that Father Paul merely retorted, "*The Lamp* is being published to throw a light," and quoted Newman's belief as his — that he had found if he used strong language people would listen.

In 1907 he again announced the Mission of the new Order of Franciscans in the Episcopal Church. "The Pope is the supreme head of the Church and I call on the Anglican Communion to repudiate the doctrine of the Reformation which denied this to the Pope."

In 1908, Church Unity Octave was observed for the first time. It was held from the Feast of Saint Peter's Chains on January 18th to the Feast of Saint Paul on January 25th. The idea had come to Father Paul from an Englishman who had suggested that it might be a good way to get popular support for his community's endeavors. He was correct, for quite spontaneously several thousands — clergy, religious, and laity — followed the Octave that first year in both Anglican and Catholic churches.

By the next year it was much better organized and had a regular program — prayers, public and private, masses and communions, sermons and conferences on church unity.

Early in 1909 there had been news of an amazing conversion to Rome — that of Henry Sargent, head of the Episcopal Order of the Holy Cross. And later in the same year came news of the reception of Father Paul's entire Society of the Atonement into the Catholic Church. It consisted at that time of two friars, five sisters, and ten tertiaries. The membership was small but the noise of their going was great indeed, and the echoes resounded for a long time in the church they had left.

The first Christmas at Graymoor after the reception

into the Catholic Church was one unlimited in its joyous celebration. The small community had two real Friars Minor with them for the midnight Mass in the convent chapel of Our Lady of the Angels. Father Godfrey was celebrant, Father Paschal was deacon, and Father Paul was sub-deacon.

They had been received as a body of religious living corporately under the Rule of Saint Francis. Now the Brothers and Sisters bound themselves to work in the future for three things : the reconciliation of sinners to God through the Blood of the Atonement; the winning of Anglicans and non-Papal Christians to the obedience of Peter ; and the conversion of the heathen.

There was no need of disbanding the organization and then re-establishing it. There were of course certain changes required because of ecclesiastical requirements. Father Paul had petitioned for admission and his work had been carefully investigated and finally approved. The two friars became real friars minor now and Father Paul was shortly after ordained a priest. One of the first converts who came to the Society was a Jew who was known in religion as Brother Anthony.

The one thing that especially pleased Father Paul was that *The Lamp* lost only a few subscriptions because of its move. There were of course indignant letters in *The Living Church*. One angry writer spoke of Father Paul's "mental processes for coming to so lamentable a position," and even claimed he had no right to the property, because, when he had gone about collecting money for his project he said he would turn it over to his own Bishop later — and now it would belong to the Roman Catholics who had utterly no right to it.

There had been, of course, a certain difficulty about the Friary's right to be where it was. But the mountain had been entirely unoccupied when Father Paul came, and no one had objected to his staying or even to his modest building. But, now, as more building was planned, as roads were being carved out of the mountain and more money would be spent for improvements, it was thought advisable to clear up the title to the property. The community knew that Hamilton Fish Sr., was one of the owners, and they went to ask if he could find out who else owned it and how much they would sell it for.

Mr. Fish investigated and told the Friars that there were several owners, and that three thousand dollars would buy the land. "Have you it ?" he asked.

Father Paul shook his head. "I haven't thirty cents," he said.

"What are you going to do about it then ?" asked the puzzled Mr. Fish, amazed at the serenity of his admittedly hopeless reply.

"Pray," said Father Paul succinctly, and left for his chapel.

Everyone prayed during that next week, the length of time allowed for payment of the sum required for a clear title to Graymoor Mountain. There was no response of a financial sort.

On the last day a man who had been interested in the Friar's work but knew nothing about this desire to buy the property, came to Father Paul with a check for five thousand dollars to help him carry on his work. And after that Graymoor Mountain belonged to the Order whose first member had long before planted a cross of cedars on its top to dedicate the place to the glory of God.

Sometimes during the first years of Father Paul's life on his mountain, tramps or stray men wandering about to get away from their troubles had found their way to him and he had housed them as best he could in the chicken house on the mountainside, still standing close to the little Friary. He called it St. Christopher's Inn and began calling the strays and vagrants his Brothers Christopher.

The chicken house is still there, and the old paint shed is preserved as part of a little chapel that stands in Graymoor woods. But not chicken house nor Friary either could hold today the Brothers Christopher who come to Graymoor, for they come in crowds now where in the old days they came singly. Any homeless man can come there for bed and meals and no question is asked except his name. In exchange the guests give whatever work they are best qualified to do. There is plenty to do, for there are hundreds who come each week. There are new buildings to put up and new roads to be made. Nearly all of it has been done by the Brothers Christopher themselves.   The Franciscan ideal is still the working plan which Father Lewis Wattson brought with him to Graymoor.

His Church Unity Octave has grown so that it is now celebrated widely throughout the country by Catholics, ever since the day in 1910 when Father Paul received with joy two letters, containing approbation of the movement.   One came from Archbishop Farley, the other from Monsignor Da Falconi, the Apostolic Delegate.

In later years the radio too was enlisted to further the work.   The Ave Maria hour, broadcast every Sunday throughout the nation, included a talk by the Founder, music, and the life of a saint in dramatic form.

Father Paul died in 1938, but the voices that are heard at Graymoor seem but a continuation of his own. His tomb is a part of what is known as Saint Anthony's Shrine, and is still only partially completed.   Around it are many buildings — the large friary, the college, the monastery, and the chicken house which sheltered the first Brothers Christopher.   In the chapel the spirit of Father Paul is everywhere, and the Friars talk of him as if he had only gone away for a little while.

He was always a true Franciscan ; he loved the poor and he was markedly ascetic.   Once a priest who planned to join the Society went to Graymoor to try it out.   He came away, however, saying he could not attain the asceticism of such a saint — "I found him sleeping on the floor of the belfry because the others needed the better places."

Father Paul worked for his Church with his hands, helping in the actual building of Graymoor. And he helped — through his sermons, through *The Lamp*, through his radio program — with his head and his heart. "He teaches us," said the Dominican who delivered his funeral sermon, "that religion can be most attractive when the instincts of a gentleman are supernaturalized."

# MARION GURNEY

## Mother Marianne of Jesus
### [1868– ]

> *"The city will be saved by
> the regeneration of human
> lives as one by one they
> are brought back to the
> Sacraments of the Church."*

One of Marion Gurney's earliest childhood recollections was that of going to church with her mother. She was just five years old, and with great dignity she carried a Book of Common Prayer in one hand and a blue parasol in the other. The church was very small and sometimes she and her mother formed the whole congregation. Suddenly there was no more minister either and the church was closed.

She remembered nothing in any way connected with religion until five years later when she was living with her family in California. One afternoon an Irish maid in the family took Marion for a walk and she took the child into a church with her. Marion was very little impressed. There was an unintelligible gabbling going on alternately between the man up in front and the people about her and it was certainly not English.

But suddenly her boredom left her at sight of a boy lighting many candles and the man who had been gabbling came out again, this time in a gleaming white cloak, and held out over the people Something white in a case of glass framed in glittering gold. With the instinct of childhood, which sometimes brings undulled perceptions to holy things, the child felt the Presence there.

She walked home, the spell still on her, and next day went to work to make her own playroom look as much as possible like the scene she had witnessed. She put in a corner the dolls and toys. She brought in masses of bright California flowers and put them around the room. She begged some candles from the cook and put them on her little nursery table, and then sat down in her chair to try to recapture that wonderful feeling she had when the gold and glass had flashed across her fascinated gaze. She sat for a long time but the feeling she had experienced in the church the day before would not come back to her.

Marion's mother had no leaning toward any special religious sect, but she felt very strongly one thing : her daughter should be left free to choose what she wanted for herself when she grew old enough to do so. As it happened, Marion had no thought of being anything but an Episcopalian. Catholicism she never gave a thought to, because for one thing she believed that it was a religion into which one was born, and that this was the only way to be one. But as she grew up, it was the Anglican Church which interested her, so much so that on her graduation from Wellesley she became for a time a novice in an Anglican convent. Her family offered strenuous objections to this course, but Marion was a determined young woman, a great deal like her ancestor

Elizabeth Fry, the English prison reformer, and she stuck to her intention until she herself realized that this was not her place in the scheme of things and she left the order.

She came back to New York City to live and became greatly interested in the settlement work of the Episcopal Church, especially the work among the children. Some friends of hers owned a piece of land up the Hudson, with old buildings on it, among them a chapel. They suggested that Miss Gurney take this property to use as a summer home for her settlement children, since the buildings were in fair enough condition for summer occupancy.

The chapel too they wanted put to use, and asked her to select a chaplain for the religious teaching of the children. Miss Gurney tackled the job bravely, knowing that the chaplain would of course have to be High Church in his beliefs. She had to catechise the various applicants for the position and get their qualifications. Some did not believe in hearing confessions and some objected to Reservation of the Sacrament and some did not want to use the word Mass as applied to the services.

Suddenly Miss Gurney realized that what she was doing was a bit odd : she was catechising her fathers in God as to just what they believed. Something was wrong about a situation like that.

On top of this disturbing thought, she heard the news that the Bishop of her diocese had announced that there should be no Reservation in any Episcopal Church of

his diocese, no matter how High its leaning. She knew
of course that this practice had been going on in several
churches and she was soon to learn it would continue,
despite the Bishop's order. She felt again some flaw in
the bright jewel of her faith.

Worried about the whole matter, she came to New
York one day for supplies for her settlement children,
and dropped into her own very liturgical church to say
a few prayers to ease her worry. Inside in the front of
the church was glowing the familiar red light and she
began to genuflect as was her invariable custom. But
try as she would she could not make the familiar gesture,
even though her will tried to force her to do it.

Bewildered, unhappy, feeling she had no spiritual home
at all, she decided to go to talk to an old friend of hers,
once an Anglican, but now a Catholic convert and a
priest. She took a cab to his rectory, the nearby one of
Saint Francis Xavier. Before calling on him she went
into his church to pray, and this time she found she had
no trouble whatever in genuflecting before the altar.
When later in the rectory of the church she told her story
to Father van Rensselaer, he smiled at her encouragingly.
"But it is not at all mysterious. Of course you belong
here. Come right in."

So she gave up the difficult problem of adjusting the
chaplain to the chapel. However, the little building
was converted from Anglicanism too, long years after
Miss Gurney made her submission to Rome. It stands
today on the grounds of Graymoor, and the Anglican

Order which took charge of it after Miss Gurney resigned her job there, came over to Rome eventually too.

When she was received into the Church, her sponsor was Mrs. William Arnold, herself a convert and a woman who through her years in the Church was to prove one of the foremost promoters of the Catholic social service in settlement houses. Through her, Marion Gurney met young Father Thuente, later Prior of Saint Vincent Ferrer's, but at that time a young priest who was meditating the almost revolutionary idea of a Catholic settlement house in his crowded foreign parish in the East Sixties.

When permission was finally granted Father Thuente offered the post to Miss Gurney. It was a crowded neighborhood — one square block of the parish held six thousand Italians and Bohemians, nearly all traditionally Catholic but fallen away from regular religious observance and attendance at church. Something must be done to get them back to their own church. When the settlement opened there were but three children in their Sunday School; a year later only two families were sending their children to a Protestant mission. The latter had been proselytizing with turkeys and new clothes and coal, but the little group at St. Catherine's soon learned that these were not necessary. All that was needed was personal kindly contact and the creating of a Catholic atmosphere to bring them back to their Church. Often the child came first and brought the parents back to their neglected faith.

"The City of New York," wrote the indignant Miss Gurney on one occasion, "will be saved not by the distribution of clothing and groceries, but by the regeneration of human lives brought back one by one to the Sacraments."

The settlement was named Saint Rose's after the Saint of Lima. Miss Gurney stayed there for some five years, long enough to get it well established. But always there was much more work to do than there were people to do it. The few priests she could call on were greatly overworked, as were the religious who could aid her. One day she came across an account of the English Confraternity of Christian Doctrine, and thought she had found an answer to her difficulties. The Confraternity was soon established at Saint Rose's with the hearty approval of Archbishop Corrigan, and there young men and women were trained to teach the children. The classes were taught by interested priests and laymen, and at the end of the two years' course the graduates received diplomas at regular graduating exercises, and were then sent to the various parishes which asked for their services.

After some years Saint Rose's was in flourishing condition. Then Miss Gurney was called home suddenly because of illness in her family. When, two years later, she came back to New York it was to face the discouraging fact that her work had all but gone to pieces. Nothing daunted, she set out to repair and to get things going again. Calling on the priests and lay people who had been her faithful aids before, and on new ones as well, she began, in her home parish of Saint Catherine of Genoa on the Upper West side, the work which was eventually to end in the foundation of her own community. She established a small house and women who became associated with her went about their Christian Doctrine work there and in other parishes in the city.

In 1910 these women came down to the Cherry Hill district, where they at first merely helped out in the parish and then, with encouragement that made the project possible, they came down to live.

By this time, too, Miss Gurney had come to the conclusion that if this idea of hers were to have permanence it must not be dependent on a few of the laity who might have to give it up at any time, but it would have to be in charge of some religious organization. She tried to persuade various communities to take up the work but no one wanted it. So finally there was nothing left for her to do but start an organization herself — and thus began the Society of the Sisters of Our Lady of Christian Doctrine. She herself took the name of Mother Marianne of Jesus.

They began to hunt around the neighborhood for a house, and they had to hunt with care for their income was very small. They opened negotiations with an old Catholic gentleman who owned a house at 173 Cherry Street. But, while they were still negotiating, some clerical relatives of his who were also friends of the new religious group, persuaded him to give the house to them instead of renting it, and he did.

There were five or six in the group when the prospect of making it a religious community began to take more definite shape, and they had the efficient aid of Father Francis McCarthy, S.J.   The little group presented their desires to ecclesiastical authorities and before long the Religious of the Society of Our Lady of Christian Doctrine was established, with its purpose the teaching of Christian doctrine and the promoting of its practice by suitable social activities.

Their director, Father McCarthy, arranged to have one of the Dominican nuns from Blauvelt come down to Cherry Hill and act as novice mistress for the new community.   More members came in and when they took their final vows in 1915, there were fifteen members, some of whom had taken temporary vows five years before.   The congregation was then canonically established by Cardinal Farley who appointed Monsignor Lavelle as ecclesiastical superior.

A hurried biographical sketch could not cover even a small part of the later work of the Sisters, but nearly all of it was interesting and difficult.   Back in 1910, social service work was not nearly so well organized as it is today, and conditions in Cherry Hill were deplorable.   It was a place regarded by authorities as one of the toughest sections of the city, a place where policemen never went singly about their duties.

There was, for instance the incident — or perhaps battle would be the better word — of one of the boys' clubs of the neighborhood.   It was called by its members 'The

Cherry Blossoms,' and it was a redoubtable group, toughest of the tough gangs who met on Cherry Hill. They came in a group to the door one evening and asked if they might use one of the rooms for their club meetings.

The Sister who met them hesitated for a moment when she heard the name, for even the police held that flower-titled group in a certain awe. But after all, she considered, that was what they had come down there for, so a room in the newly opened Madonna House was assigned to them. It was equipped with an old piano, chairs and a table. The meeting took place, and before the evening was over the Cherry Blossoms had completely demolished the piano (the Sisters had to admit complete destruction as they viewed the strings sticking sadly up in the air through the broken case) and the chairs, the window panes, and the chandelier were likewise completely smashed.

Being hardy characters, the Sisters decided to ignore this unusual form of meeting, and when the gang came back the next week, Mother Marianne explained that they had no more furniture to give them now, except a table, because the boys themselves had wrecked the room's entire equipment. It seemed to make little difference to the boys, however, and they prepared to go ahead with their meeting.

Later in the evening the Sisters decided it might be a good idea to bring in several pies they had left from supper as refreshments. When the boys saw these, it seemed to be a signal for every Cherry Blossom to seize some portion of the pies and to throw them at each other and at the walls. Then they went home after a thoroughly amusing evening, and the Sisters, though they did not especially enjoy having their pies used as missiles, said nothing but merely cleaned up the place. For the next week they had enlisted the services of a tall, athletic youth who arrived promptly to take the group in charge. But instead the boys took him aside and after a brief talk he came to the Sisters and told them he really valued his life and thought he would not stay to help. He departed in haste, glancing behind him nervously until the house was out of sight.

But the next week a treasure appeared, a middle-aged man of no particularly athletic build, who had heard of their troubles and offered to help. He evidently understood boys, for from that time the Cherry Blossom meetings ran with more smoothness and no more destruction of property. As the years passed it became a pattern club and dropped its name for that of the Saint Aloysius Guild.

The man who understood boys engaged them in athletic exercises and when one of the boys asked if they might drill he brought wooden guns and drilled them himself. When the war broke out the Guild became the Columbus Volunteers of New York, and 711 members of the group went into service for their country. The Club remained in existence after the war, and members are still drilling at Madonna House, officered by veterans of the war. They have been invaluable in their work among the young men of the district.

There was, as the years passed, happiness in Mother Marianne's heart as she saw the lengthening line of boys and girls reclaimed to the great reality of their own Faith. It was the greatest evidence that the work of her Sisters was needed.

The work goes on busily today. Madonna House still functions on the teeming East Side. The Sisters conduct a Christian Doctrine class on Saturdays for over two hundred children. There is a Greek social club that takes care of Greek mothers and children, and a Newman Club for young men attending the public school, this latter offering vocational training for its members. One of the most interesting phases of their work is one recently undertaken : between forty and fifty Chinese children are under instruction there with the co-operation of the Maryknoll Fathers.

Every week at least five thousand people pass the doors of Madonna House, which is no longer a single building but occupies four whole buildings on Cherry and Market Streets. It carries on an elaborate program of religious, cultural, and recreational activities and serves the social needs of its neighbors literally from cradle to grave. Of the twenty proselyting agencies at work among the Catholic population when the Sisters came, one of them used to encourage the children to come to its doors instead of to the little Catholic mission by having one of its members stand in the street and wave new clothing invitingly at the children going past, many have been closed and the rest but sparsely attended. The Sisters brought the children back to their Church and they keep them there.

Madonna House recently reported that fifteen different nationalities were represented in one of its classes, among them Italian, Spanish, Lithuanian, Greek, Jewish, Albanian, and American Negro.

At the head of it still moves Mother Marianne, born Marion Gurney, who leads a busy life between her convent at Nyack and Madonna House.

She has seen to it that the liturgy has a proud place in her Order. All her convent chapels are perfectly liturgical and the services of the Church are carried out in the full flower of their beauty. Despite the exceptionally busy life which the Sisters lead, the Divine Office (not the Little Office) is recited every day in the choir.

Mother Marianne deserves honor for the development of the work in Christian Doctrine which she has effected, and especially for having shown its great practical use in Catholic Action. Her early methods are still used in the community's work, though modified by being kept abreast of modern pedagogy. The use of pictures, symbols, music, drama, and liturgy are all freely employed and no reward or other incentives have been needed to secure the attendance. The child is taught to apply the teachings of his Faith to his actual problems in the world, and then the whole is so linked with the liturgical year

that the recurring seasons constantly renew the memory
of these lessons.

There is one other task Mother Marianne has set for
herself and her Sisters : to claim for God some of the
leisure which, instead of being a boon to young people,
is so often a menace instead.  The Sisters offer, therefore, a wide variety of occupations, both cultural and
recreational, suited to different ages and temperaments
and degrees of intelligence and they are always watching
and hoping that each student will find and develop some
absorbing hobby as a means of self-expression and a safe-
guard against the many pitfalls of modern life.

During her busy life, Mother Marianne has dealt in
great measure with corporal works of mercy, with feeding and clothing and housing those who need it.  But,
along with the feeding of the body, she has made it her
special work to teach God's word, and so bring food for
the soul as well as for the body to the children of poverty
and neglect.  She gives to our Lord's small ones that
sense of the wonderful Presence which a little girl met
with long ago in a Catholic Church and which she, grown
to womanhood, found again and realized she must make
known to other children in all its value and necessity.

# WILMOTH ALEXANDER FARMER

## Francis X. Farmer, S.J.
## [1877–    ]

> *"Only follow at any cost,*
> *a great reward awaits you."*

The story of Wilmoth Alexander Farmer, Methodist missionary from Kentucky, later the Reverend Francis X. Farmer, S.J., came to light in a small brown paper bound book which bore the imprint of the T'ou-Sè-Wè Press of Shanghai. It arrived in the mail from some missioner in China who was sending the booklet along with his appeal for help with his mission.

The book was entitled *My Conversion,* and the frontispiece was a small photograph of the author. It was a face which, were it not for the biretta, would be exactly the popular idea of a Protestant minister. The names given as his baptismal names were Francis Xavier, and it was obvious on reading the story, that these were not the names his family gave him in his childhood baptism. Little by little the story was unwound, mainly with the help of a book he had written when he was still a Methodist missionary.

Wilmoth Farmer was born in Georgia in 1877, but spent most of his boyhood in Covington, Kentucky. The family had been Methodist for generations, and, although the father had no church affiliation Wilmoth's mother was a devout church woman. One of his earliest memories was seeing her, after she had heard his own prayers and tucked him into bed, kneeling before the fireplace, still and recollected in her own prayers. Night after night he went to sleep with his last waking picture the figure of his mother, in the flickering firelight, her face tranquil, her eyes closed, her hands devoutly folded.

As for himself, he could not remember a time when he did not love God, due to his mother's loving teaching and example. And when he was twelve years old, he begged to be allowed to join her church and was permitted to do so.

When he had finished high school, he went to Emory College near Covington, a Methodist institution. Here he helped with the revival work and the other church activities expected from the students. He read a great deal in the school library which was well supplied with devotional literature, and, when the time of his graduation arrived, he knew what he meant to make his life work : he wanted to be a minister of the gospel.

His father, who had planned to make a good business man out of his son, felt some annoyance when he heard of his son's own plans, but at last, seeing how much his wife desired it, he agreed to finance Wilmoth's further studies at Vanderbilt University. Here he met an earnest group of young men who had organized themselves into a mission at the Old Tulip Street Church in Nashville and were busy with plans for foreign missionary work, a project which appealed to their young idealism and in which he enlisted eagerly.

The following year Wilmoth's father received news which was even worse than the other had been. It was bad enough for his son to be a minister, but now he was told that Wilmoth wanted to go to the foreign mission field. Again, however, he yielded, and young Farmer spent some time in preparation at the Missionary Training Institute at Nyack, New York, under the auspices of the Methodist Missionary Alliance.

Early in 1901 he sailed for China. He had very definite designs for his work there, and one of them was that, in order to reach as many people as possible, he would live as nearly like the Chinese as possible. He worked hard to acquire some knowledge of their language, and while doing so, he took on their customs and dress also, and he seasoned his role by wearing an elegant cue, and by eating only native food. He preached, distributed tracts, and was as happy as he was busy, sure in his belief that he had found the life God meant him to lead.

In the following year he was introduced to an attractive young woman, Ada Beeson, who had recently arrived in China as a missionary, having just graduated from the Institute in Nyack where he had spent the previous year. She was a Southerner, from Alabama, one of the eleven children of a pious Methodist home, who had been converted to Christ in the usual Methodist way when she was a young girl and who, after a few years as school teacher, had felt the desire to be a foreign missionary. Like young Farmer, she had definite ideas as to what her work was to be : she wanted to get in touch with Chinese women, and when she met Wilmoth she was already deep in the study of the Mandarin language.

One of the rules of the Mission which was supporting their work was that the missionaries had to work in the field for two years before they could marry, but there was never any doubt in Ada's mind that she had found her future husband. Her brother had said to her that he was willing to have her go to China — "if there were any young men there." Now she wrote him happily, "Well, the only one I ever loved is here and I am very happy in it all, for I believe it is God's Will." Besides long ago she had made a vow : she would never marry anyone but a missionary.

In 1904 they were married, and in Chinese wedding costumes. It was a good idea, Farmer thought, for it would help remove the fear and prejudice of "foreign devils." And then he would not have to cut off his cue either.

They were sent to a mission where they could work together, and had an exciting time getting to their station. It was called P'ing Loh — in English, Tranquil Joy, a name that seemed a good omen to the pair. One night of their journey was spent at a Chinese inn, where the old lady who owned it insisted on putting the chickens under their bed at night. Exhausted with preaching and tract distributing on the way, they had to listen to cocks crowing at various hours of the early morning. At another stopping-place they found several farm animals in their room when they awoke.

To begin mission work at P'ing Loh was not easy. There had never been a white man there so Ada had agreed for Wilmoth to leave her at another station while he went ahead to house-hunt. He finally managed to rent a house, a miserable, dirty place with bare earth walls, covered with moss, ferns and cobwebs. But after he had whitewashed the old house, he brought her there, to the excitement of the whole town which was on the *qui vive* to see the foreign devil woman. They both scrubbed and cleaned, filled lamps, and settled the few pieces of furniture and wedding presents they had brought with them. Then, recorded Ada in her diary, "He read to me while I mended. We studied Romans on Sanctification."

The young missionaries had asked for and received a military escort, both for safety and to make an impression. Even so, there was trouble at first, for some of the Chinese tried to keep others from coming to the new mission, using such fearsome arguments as that the foreign devils would cut out the children's eyes.

But before long the young missionaries had won a measure of approval. Ada was so pleasant with the women, so willing to go into the straw huts of the poor as well as in the reception parlors of the wealthy, that she soon had children coming to the Mission. They called her "Mrs. Flower."

The first Christmas they would have been very lonely for home, had they not had each other. They found some red berries that looked almost like holly and decorated the house with them, and in the old wine brewery which Wilmoth had rented and turned into a chapel they held the old church services of home.

They spent their vacations with friends in Macao, and in 1906 they were sent back to the United States on furlough. When they returned they were sent to Liucheo-Si. Wilmoth again went ahead to find a house ; again there was the fear and the hate ; the military escort, the trouble in getting a chapel.

In this city Ada began plans for carrying out her great dream : an industrial school for girls. She gave this all the time she could spare from the teaching in the mission and the care of her house — a damp, ugly place whose bare, uninviting rooms she had made cosy and homelike with her deft hands. They were the only two white people in the city.

During that year she coaxed the children to come to the mission and learn to sing hymn tunes, and by the year's end was able to chronicle in her diary "forty present."

Wilmoth meantime had the harder mission work — the services, the actual work of building, the training of those whom he had converted to become aids and catechists. In April of 1907 they sailed for home again, for Wilmoth was ill and in need of a rest. Ada was going home for another reason : she was to have a baby. But she hated to leave her work, and knelt in prayer on the little boat, weeping as the city faded from their sight.

It was wonderful to be home — to see their loved ones again, and they felt a deep patriotism stir in them when the ship touched the shores of America.

Then came great sorrow, for the little son died after but two days of life, living only long enough to let his parents know how much they loved him. Wilmoth was especially sad for his wife, thinking how much time she had given to loving other people's children and how she had looked forward to one of her own.

He put the baby on the bed beside her for a moment, dressed for his burial in one of the dresses she had made for him. "But he looks as if he were only asleep," she said to her husband almost in disbelief.

"Hopes and cherished plans of months," wrote Wilmoth later, "nailed inside a small casket."

When she recovered, they both went to speak at various conventions and missionary meetings and then prepared to return to their work. This time Wilmoth's mother could not bear to have them go. She bore up bravely until they left, but their last glimpse was of her weeping bitterly and bent with grief. She had wanted them to stay longer, but they could not. "We must go home," they said. And home was China.

They went back with more money to work with this time, and Ada had been definitely promised the funds for her industrial school. Wilmoth was busy with plans for a new memorial chapel.

During the following year Ada began to grow thinner and spoke of feeling weak. And it was not from work, for there were more missionaries on the station now to help them. She spoke of her weariness with annoyance for she was too busy to be ill. She set to work, while in bed for a while, on her conference paper of the year's work. But by summer the willing hands had grown too tired to serve, the feet that for years had run errands for others dragged at their work. The struggle against exhausting odds in the little mission stations, the primitive conditions, had worn her down, and finally an attack of dysentery decided Wilmoth to take her to Hongkong where it was much cooler. He went back to Liucheo — "the first time I have ever left her behind," said his diary. But she told him she would wait and pray and hear God's will. She sent Christmas gifts home, meanwhile, and bought things for her own house — a good foreign cooking stove, her first in China — matting, two new chairs. She wrote Wilmoth she felt like a bride making her first plans.

Early in October she insisted on returning : she must be there by October 14, Wilmoth's birthday. She was very ill now and an American friend came to nurse her. Her family wanted her sent home but she was too far gone for so long a voyage.

Wilmoth used to listen for her voice when he came home, and when he heard her singing hymns to herself, he knew she was feeling better. Later she could only hum them, in a voice too weak to sing.

In the middle of March, Wilmoth knew she was dying and one evening when he went in to her room he asked, "Ada, do you know you are going home ?"

"Yes, I am so happy," she said.

"Ada dear, you will see our little son soon."

The emaciated face brightened. "Yes, yes, he is so sweet."

She put her little hands, clammy with coming death, around his neck and summoned strength to draw his face to hers and kiss him.

He looked at her through his tears, "Ada, do you know why I am crying ?"

She nodded weakly. "Yes — because you love me." She did not speak again until late in the evening. Then she whispered to him, "I was never disobedient to the heavenly vision," and he assured her she had never been.

Next morning she died. The Christian Chinese women brought orange blossoms and roses to cover her casket. When her funeral services were read in the chapel, everyone wore white as a symbol of mourning. Her burial on a hill in a foreign land was, thought Wilmoth, like that of Sarah of old, buried in Canaan by Abraham. But why did God take her, he wondered, when Liucheo needed her, and the chapel and the school needed her — and he did too — why was it that all the prayers sent up for her went unanswered ? Then he comforted himself : of course they were answered — but in God's way. She had, he thought, like Henry Martyn, "burned out for God."

A month after her death, he sailed for a vacation at home and the most cherished possessions he took with him were her diaries and manuscript paper, and especially one photograph of her, on which she had written, "only follow at any cost, a great reward awaits you."

All this was saved from destruction in a storm when, two days after the ship *Asia* left Hong Kong, she was wrecked. Wilmoth lost everything else but he saved Ada's papers and her picture. He felt it was a call from God to write the book of her life. When he reached home, his mother encouraged him in the work and saw to it that he had plenty of leisure for rest and retirement to get over his deep sorrow by writing the memoir.

He wrote the book through blinding tears of grief and anguish. He would have liked to write much more of her as wife and helpmate, but he felt it should be especially about her religious and missionary life — the story of the missionary life that is no romance but plain, hard, monotonous, seldom heroic, but full of plain everyday duties for Christ. He wanted to tell how she fasted once every week, as was an old Methodist custom in her family, and adhered to it without fail in China. When the book was finished and published, he went back to China again.

He was very lonely now, with Ada gone. He went his accustomed way, preaching, baptizing, celebrating the Lord's Supper, travelling miles in his mission barque. And, in the dreary torrential seasons, he began to devote his spare time to reading, especially to the reading of theology, for he had felt for years that his university courses had not given him nearly enough.   And now, as a man of forty, he found he was reading in a very different way than had the youth of twenty.

In the course of reading the books he had brought with him from the United States, he came across a baffling statement : never in the course of his later life could Martin Luther be brought to deny the Real Presence in the Blessed Sacrament.   As he read that, he suddenly thought : what if the Roman view is the right one ?

For a Methodist missionary this was a truly terrifying thought and he tried to put it from him.   But as he read more he found himself dissenting frequently from the Methodist statements he read, and he began to see with surprise and dismay that the Protestant Reformation had certain ugly aspects and glaring inconsistencies.   He felt compromised, unhappy, and his preaching to his Chinese Christians became more and more difficult for him.   Besides they often asked him why there was this puzzling division in Christian life, these wrangling sects.   And he saw that interchurch movements, meant to give Protestantism cohesion, always collapsed.   Over and over, one thought went drumming through his head : they could not all be true or authoritative.   Perhaps the hated old citadel did hold the divine deposit of the Christian faith. To him the Church of Rome had been a cult, a superstition, a Gargantuan moral system almost pagan in principle.   But the years of difficult mission work had given him a riper, soberer appraisal of doctrinal problems.

Finally he sent to England for two volumes by John Henry Newman, the *Apologia* and *The Development of Christian Doctrine* and when he had finished reading them, he knew that the evidence he had hoped to push from him was overwhelming. He knew he himself was nothing more than a heretic. He now saw, finally and irrevocably, that there had been only one Christian Church — the Church of Rome.

He could not visit a Catholic priest in this dilemma, for his Methodist confrères would have been angry. As it was, when he let slip a word or two now and then about Catholicism, they were irritated at his interest in such a topic. In 1914, instead of going for the hot season to the mountains with the others, he went to Shanghai and there visited the Catholic rectory and asked to see the pastor. Father Peter Bornand S.J., to whom he spoke frankly of his problem, gave him some books to read, talked with him, and in subsequent visits explained the catechism to him in a simple way, just as Farmer had been wont to explain Methodism to his converts.

He went back to the mission with a burdened heart. And there he was greeted with what, under the circumstances, seemed a final blow. He was told that he was being offered an excellent new position — a professorship in the Protestant University at Nanking, where members of various sects came, each to study his own tenets, but where all together were to work in the interests of a common Protestantism. This was a big promotion, and he now had to face the making of a definite decision. He knew his family would be heartbroken when they heard of the step he was contemplating ; his friends would turn from him. Yet how could he take the university offer in good conscience, and how could he refuse it without an explanation ?

Finally he went to his Bishop and poured out the whole story, to the great astonishment of that official, who was kindness itself to the distraught man and strove to draw him away from this viewpoint, suggesting finally that he go home for awhile and rest. His salary would be continued ; he could come back when he had recovered.

So, on leave of absence, he sailed for home, but first he went to Shanghai to see Father Bornand once more. "I am almost losing my mind over this problem," he told him.

Father Bornand smiled at him reassuringly, "Don't fear. God will never desert you."

He took the distressed man into the church and taught him for the first time how to make the sign of the cross and genuflect before the Tabernacle.

"And now let us pray a moment, as we have the Blessed Lord with us always here," he said as they knelt there together. He sped him on his way with his blessing.

Wilmoth Farmer packed his clothing and his personal effects to take with him. His books he planned to leave, but as he put them carefully in boxes, he realized that he was doing it with the thought that they could be readily shipped to him, if he did not return. And in his heart he knew he would not come back, that his work in China was ended. His old traditions were slipping from him like a vaporous dream — his youthful idealism, his life long friends, his years of work in the missions.

He had half hoped that when he got to Shanghai, the old influences and his ministerial confrères would steady him and bring him back. He had written his mother of his troubles, and also a few devoted friends, and now pathetically tender letters were coming from home. To his mother he had written very freely of what was in his mind, of how he felt Protestantism was merely a negative faith, of how the divine magnetism and logic of the ancient Catholic teaching was swaying him.

Among the pictures he packed to take with him was the one of Ada under which she had written, "Only follow at any cost, a great reward awaits you." It was like a personal message from the person who had understood him best of all because she loved him most.

At Honolulu he met a Belgian religious to whom he spoke of his problem, and who gave him Father Conway's *Question Box* to read on the ship. And he, who had read steadily and thoroughly the great doctrinal chapters of Newman and the epic of his doubts and conversions, found here the answers to the questions he had been asking — the hackneyed objections of Protestantism against Rome as answered for the man in the street.

Back home in Covington, he was warmly greeted by relatives and friends. But his mother's eyes were worried as she looked at his thin, drawn face. On his first Sunday at home, she came to ask him if he were going to church with her. He shook his head, and saw the look of fear in her eyes.

When she had gone — to pray for him he knew — he left the house for the Sacred Heart Church near his home. He entered with a certain assurance now, made the sign of the cross and genuflected. Kneeling there, he remembered Father Bornand's quiet voice saying, "Let us pray for a moment as we have the Blessed Lord always with us here."

He had bought, too, the *Imitation of Christ* — not the Protestant version this time, the only one he had previously known, but the one which contained the chapters on the Real Presence and Holy Communion from which John Wesley had carefully protected his followers.

One day Farmer went to see an old friend to whom he opened his heart about everything. In answer to the serious difficulties he presented, he received only sarcasm and ridicule. Still, even though he was deeply hurt, he knew that by engaging in such discussion, he was himself merely dodging an issue that must, sooner or later, be faced.

Two months after he came home he had definitely made up his mind. He severed his connection with the Methodist Mission Board and sent his credentials of ordination to his Bishop.

He went back to the Sacred Heart Church, this time to see the pastor and tell him of his intentions. Through him, Farmer was put in touch with Bishop Keily of Savannah, who proved the good friend he sorely needed at that point in his life. At the Bishop's invitation he went to visit him in Savannah, and on the way stopped off to present a letter from Father Bornand to the Jesuit Fathers at Macon. The religious life of the sons of Ignatius held him from the first — the order, the holy silence at the presence of God, the spiritual joy, the intense devotion to Our Lord and to His Mother. He thought of Jacob's cry after his night at Bethel: "This is no other but the House of God and the Gate of Heaven." Here, he felt, if it could be brought to pass, would be his home.

The news that had struck his home like a thunderbolt had not yet spent its force, for it was a group entrenched in Protestantism for many generations.

"My son," his mother pleaded with him, "wait till I am dead before you become a Catholic priest."

He looked at her, deep worry in his eyes. "But what if I feel it would be a sin against the Holy Ghost?"

After that she said little to oppose him. And, when a friend came to console her some years later and spoke in anger about Wilmoth's defection, she shook her head. "I feel certain that my son though a Catholic and a priest, is fulfilling God's will in China."

Before he left Savannah he had been received into the Church and had received Holy Communion for the first time in May 1915. After his reception he remained quietly at home for a time, letting his body rest and filling his heart and soul with this new life in God.

Some months later he fulfilled the hope he had first held in Savannah and became a Jesuit. Since, however, he wanted to go back again to work in China, to teach truth there now, as he put it, instead of confusion, he became a member of the French Province of the Jesuits. That country he felt was his field of work in the future as it had been in the past, and he was eager to return.

For many years he has labored in Shanghai, as assistant in the Church of the Sacred Heart, and during the last four years he has been its pastor. The church was built in 1874 by pioneer French Jesuit missionaries, and is located in the northeast part of the city, the section once called the American Concession and later incorporated into the International Settlement. The parish at present is really international too. There are thousands of Chinese in it, but many Japanese also, some Portuguese, and at least a few of nearly every nationality in the world, and the Sacred Heart Church is the center of the Apostolate of Prayer for the foreigners of the city and also cares yearly for hundreds of destitute Chinese families. Its Saint Vincent de Paul organization cares for the indigent foreigners. Six thousand children attend the schools of the parish, two thirds of them non-Catholics.

In 1934, Father Farmer left the Shanghai parish temporarily to do missionary work in Japan, so that he might master the language, knowledge of which has proved very useful now that he is back at Sacred Heart Church.

He sometimes tells people who ask about his personal history that he is like three sides of an equilateral triangle. His origins and education have been entirely

American; his later studies and priestly mission labors
have been with the French Jesuits; and his life consecration is with the people of his adoption — the Chinese
race.   What makes Father Farmer's conversion outstanding is the fact that he came alone to the Church.   In
Christian countries conversion is a simple matter : one
is surrounded by believers, and even though there may
be difficulties in the path there is a community solidarity
which this lonely man in China did not have.   He had
only books and a heart open to do what God wanted him
to do.   He worked through alone to the Church.   He
came there the hardest way of all — not even with opposition, for he could only oppose his arguments to himself.   Often for many converts Catholicism is perhaps
made too easy.   His case was not one of those.

All American missionaries whose travels take them to
Shanghai know Father Farmer, a genial, sunny man, still
an indefatigable mission worker whose personality attracts
both foreigners and natives.   He still has in him the sense
of hospitality of the old South where he was reared and
so proves an excellent host for tired wanderers.

The Protestant missionaries remember him, too, and
the old rancor caused by his leaving them has gone.   For
thirteen years he had gone through the East, preaching
like a good revivalist in crowded Chinese country settle-
ments where no white man had ever been, and organizing
mission points which still flourish today though he himself has gone a different way.

The little story of his conversion has been translated

into French, Italian, German, Chinese and other tongues.

"Only follow at any cost, a great reward awaits you," Ada had written on the picture of herself, and he had carried out the first portion of that counsel.    Now, in his adopted land, he is seeking the great award of souls won to God.

He has only one regret about his life and that he feels can be best expressed in the lovely words of Saint Augustine : "Too late have I loved Thee, O Beauty so ancient, O Beauty so new."

# SELDEN PEABODY DELANY
## [1874–1935]

*"In the Pope you see in the
flesh the Apostolicity of the
Church."*

On June 24, 1930, the New York papers carried the
news of the reception into the Church of Selden Peabody
Delany, rector of the Protestant Episcopal Church of
Saint Mary the Virgin. It was news which caused amazement and consternation among many of his friends, for
he had told very few of his leanings or of his intentions.
He had wanted to be very sure of his course before he
made the move or talked about it, for he felt deeply his
responsibility towards the many people who depended on
him for spiritual guidance.

Up to that time his life had followed the pattern of
many of the present day High Church clergy — a Catholicity of intent and a belief like that of the earlier Newman in the Anglican Church as a *via media* and as part of
the ancient and still living Church.

Selden Delany was born in Fond du Lac, Wisconsin,
in 1874, and was brought up in the Presbyterian Church.
While a student at Harvard, he had taken as an elective in
his junior year a course in the history of the first Christian
centuries. He noted with some surprise that the early
church bore little relation to the Presbyterian Christianity
in which he had been reared. For a thesis in this course
he was asked to write on the epistles of Saint Ignatius in

their bearing on the early church organization, and he was so surprised at what he read that he began discussing it with a classmate who invited him to come to talk the matter over further with some clergymen he knew at the Church of the Advent, a very High Church, and in the charge of the American branch of the English Cowley Fathers.

From that time on Selden Delany considered himself an Anglo-Catholic, and from that time he felt he had a vocation to the priesthood. He studied three years at the Western Theological Seminary in Chicago, and in December of 1899 he was ordained at the Cathedral in Fond du Lac. After two years as curate in smaller churches, he was made rector at Appleton, Wisconsin. Here he was able to give his High Church ambitions full sway, for his parishioners liked him very much and allowed him to do exactly as he pleased with regard to incense and flowers, and even allowed him to put a confessional in the new church they were building when he came. (When he left them they promptly took it out, having no further use for it.) During his years in Appleton he often made purchases at a little variety shop where one of the daughters of the proprietor showed him her early attempts at fiction writing. He assured young Edna Ferber that he thought her work quite promising and urged her to go ahead and write more.

In 1908, he was made dean of the Cathedral in Milwaukee and was there until 1915 when his old friend Dr. Barry, rector of the church of Saint Mary the Virgin, persuaded him to come to New York as his associate rector. During his years in New York he was editor of the erudite *American Church Monthly*.

Saint Mary's has long been noted as one of the most ritualistic of the Episcopal churches of the metropolitan district. In its general appearance and services it is almost indistinguishable from any Roman Catholic church. More than one Catholic has unwittingly gone there not aware that he was in the wrong place until he heard English instead of Latin from the altar! The church lists its services as "masses," its confessionals are conventionally Catholic, and its liturgical observances are dignified and full of the ancient beauty of the early church.

The one thing Saint Mary's has never accepted is the Pope, and Dr. Delany acquiesced in this. When asked to define his own position he was wont to say that he believed in Catholicism without the Pope. He remarked later that sometimes when he said this he was half aware of thinking inside that it was really like playing Hamlet with Hamlet left out. Thus when he felt uneasy he was apt to reassure himself by saying that his position was that of the Orthodox churches after all, and therefore he too was a part of primitive Christianity as they were.

All told he spent thirty years in the ministry of the Episcopal Church. During those years he saw many things that seemed not quite reasonable and sometimes not quite honest. He saw the men he liked best and knew best trying to live and act like Catholic priests. He saw them "walking one way with their faces turned in another direction." He saw there was no authority to uphold the Catholic way in his communion. He saw that he and the rest had to resort to Roman handbooks on confession and other doctrinal subjects, for his denomination had very few. He found he had to use Roman Catholic books of devotion continually and once called it, with some bitterness, "borrowing from a rich neighbor." He saw that every clergyman was really a law unto himself and arranged matters in his own church as he wished. And he saw that though he had been taught to be anti-papal, there was even a small group in his own communion who fought for complete reunion with Rome, admitting the Pope as the supreme authority.

As the years went by he felt his position more and more insecure. He saw how very Protestant most of his communion really were, and wondered why one should keep on with High Church practices when for those who did not want a Protestant church, there was a perfectly good Catholic church around almost any corner. During the years, too, some of his own flock became Roman Catholics. And he felt that the arguments he had used to hold them from Rome had not the logic he wished they had. And if by preaching good Catholicism he was guiding some of these sheep to the fold of Peter in an indirect fashion, as some who sympathized with his dilemma assured him, why, if there was only one true fold, should he himself remain outside it all of his life?

When his parishioners coming home from abroad asked him if, when the only Episcopal church was a very low one, it was all right for them to go to a Roman church for Mass — what was he to tell them?

In the United States and in his summer vacations in Europe he saw Catholic churches packed on Sundays for Mass after Mass. In his own church he saw a small congregation of faithful souls come to the early "mass" and a crowded church at eleven o'clock or "high mass." Why? Because that was the hallowed hour for a Protestant church service, and also because St. Mary's had an exceptional choir and an organist renowned throughout New York.

But he had many reasons for hesitating until he was very sure. He knew that his going would hurt the Catholic cause in his communion, not because of his personal importance, but because he had been a rector for many years and felt he had a duty to perform : the leading of his parishioners to become more truly Catholic. He saw how the Anglican religious orders were distrusted by most of the laity. He saw how one group used the Book of Common Prayer faithfully, and another ignored it and used books of devotion based on Roman Catholic devotional works. He saw how hampered and restricted the Catholic-minded clergy were by their bishops. And he began to see more and more clearly that what he had thought a main stream with living water was only a small waterway with no real outlet to the sea.

In 1928 he began work on a book. He had written many others but this was to be a very different one, for with each chapter which he wrote he found himself a little further from his own communion and a little nearer the Catholic Church.   As he reached the final chapter he saw more and more clearly the road he must take.   Gaily, but with heartbreak behind the words, for he knew what the cost of his defection would no doubt be, he wrote, "Many a time in my ministry I have felt the attraction of Rome but I soon got over it.   Now it is different.   This is no passing fancy.   I have lost my heart."

But first he spoke to Dr. Barry about his difficulties. The latter had retired completely two years before, and Dr. Delany had been elected rector of Saint Mary's.   He went to see his old friend at Kingston where he was in a convalescent home, and told him that he felt he must resign his charge, that in fact he was planning to do so in November, a month away.   Dr. Barry was so upset by the news that it seemed a really dangerous thing to insist on it, and with some reluctance Dr. Delany promised to wait until Dr. Barry could prepare for him arguments as to why he should not take such a step.

The arguments soon came — long typewritten pages of them, and Dr. Delany went patiently through them all. They were of course the very arguments he had himself used for years and now there seemed no logic in them at all.   Mainly of course they were arguments against the Petrine tradition, for this was one matter on which Dr. Barry felt strongly.   He absolutely denied the need of a Pope or the necessity for Rome as a city or a church.

But the year before Dr. Delany had stood in Saint

Peter's and read the words at the base of the dome : *Tu es Petrus*. And as he stood there he had felt something in his inner consciousness that shook the foundations of his life. Later that summer he had felt it again — that queer unrest, that overmastering feeling that was almost like a summons — at Lisieux.

As he read the stanchly written arguments of his friend, he remembered the Harvard thesis on Saint Ignatius. He recalled the letters the Saint wrote which so clearly showed that he admitted the precedence of the Roman community in the circle of her sister cities. He remembered others he had read — Irenaeus and Cyprian. And in Harnack's work on the *History of the Dogma* he had found that Protestant author showing clearly how much had come from the church at Rome — the New Testament canon, the Apostles' Creed, the traditional form of the apostolic ministry. Dr. Barry's chief criticism had been that the organization of the church had not been developed at Rome — yet everything Dr. Delany now read seemed to be proving the contrary.

In 1927 in London he had listened to Vernon Johnson, the noted Anglo-Catholic monk of the Society of the Divine Compassion, give a talk in Albert Hall that held ten thousand people breathless for a whole hour. Now he heard that Father Vernon had become a Catholic and he read his little book, *One Lord, One Faith*, a simple essay, written mainly to explain to the Anglo-Catholic people who loved him why he was taking this step away from their communion.   It had a strong emotional appeal for Dr. Delany, for it was so very exactly what he felt and what he himself wanted to say.

He came at last to consider the one important question — that of Anglican orders and their validity.   After reading and after prayer, he decided that his conclusion was that of the papal contention in the famous Encyclical on Anglican Orders ; that at the Reformation the Anglican Church had intentionally departed from the historical Catholic concept of the ministry.   Father Woodlock's little volume — *Constantinople, Canterbury, and Rome* gave his heart the consolation he needed, for the Jesuit said that even though the church he had served for so long had not the Real Presence, that though the Sacrament he had adored so long was only a wafer of flour and water, yet the devotion, the love, the prayers and fastings, the desire to make God's house more beautiful and the ceremonies more seemly — all these things must surely have brought an outpouring of grace on those who administered them and those to whom they were administered.

He resolved one thing : he would finish his book entirely before he made any change.   If he could still remain where he was conscientiously he must do so.   But one by one as he wrote, the arguments had broken to pieces in his hands.   And when he finished his argument for the validity of Anglican Orders, he saw one fact and only one before him : he was not a priest, he had never been a priest !

He called on a Catholic friend of his, Father Ford,

chaplain of Columbia University, and told him his decision.  An interview was arranged with Cardinal Hayes, who told him what further steps to take.

He resigned his parish and wrote a note to Dr. Barry, from whom came no answer either then or at any time in the future.  He wrote to Bishop Manning that he was renouncing the ministry of the Episcopal Church, and then left for a retreat at the Benedictine Priory at Portsmouth, Rhode Island.

Dom Leonard, who had once been Henry Sargent of the Protestant Order of the Holy Cross, gave him instruction.  On his birthday, the Feast of Saint John the Baptist, he was received into the Catholic Church by Monsignor McMahon in the Church of Our Lady of Lourdes in New York City.

He made ready to study for the priesthood at the Beda College in Rome, and reached Italy in September 1930, planning to remain there four full years.  It had been suggested that he could prepare himself in a shorter time, since he had studied Catholicism so deeply, but he felt he needed all the full course before he was ready to undertake the shepherding of a flock.  "They are necessary," he wrote, "not merely to learn something and to unlearn what is wrong, but to develop slowly but surely the character and mental outlook and spiritual habits that a Catholic priest ought to have.  I thank God daily for sending me to Rome and the Beda to form my mind and make over my life."

He came among the seminarians at the Beda as a stu-

dent and nothing more, though of course his presence
caused something of a sensation among them. "Out of
that applauding world he came to us," said an editorial
written after his death in the *Beda Review*, "and lived
with us a life not easily understood by all, because it was
a life hidden with Christ in God."

That first Christmas in Rome he served as acolyte at
the Midnight Mass in the little college chapel. The year
before, clad in white and gold vestments, he had been
celebrant at a great service in the New York church, at a
high altar lighted by many candles, the scent of flowers
and incense about him, singing the stately ritual that was
patterned so closely after that of the Catholic service.
In a letter to friends at home he wrote, "My Christmas
here is a great contrast to New York. Instead of hearing
a hundred confessions and singing the Midnight Mass
(as I thought) I make my own confession and Communion (and am sure) as one among many. Last year
the pomp and circumstance — this year sternly simple
with plainsong music. I made my first Christmas Communion. I prefer the more obscure role. But the tears
would come."

He grew to love the life at the Beda and wrote joyously
of it to friends at home. "It is a great place, just the
kind I needed at this crisis in my life. For a long time
I had been growing lukewarm through the comfortable
life I was leading — too much of the good things of the
world. Here I find the stiffening that is good for the
soul." Then, with a touch of the invincible humor which

was always a part of his baggage through life, he added,
"I forgot to mention that among our hardships we have
the most delicious wine for dinner and supper.   I don't
see how I stand it.   And we never go out in the evenings.
For years it had been my ambition to stay home evenings.
Another dream realized."

After being present for the first time at the Pope's Mass,
he wrote home, greatly stirred : "What made it so deeply
moving to me was the consciousness that I was in communion with the reigning pontiff.   I belong to him and
he belongs to me.   It is inspiring ; other values of Catholicism are more abstract or diffuse but in the Pope you see
in the flesh the Apostolicity of the Church — all given
concrete reality in this one man."

Within a year of his conversion he knew by name
seventy of his old parishioners who had followed him
into the Church, and much of his very heavy mail dealt
with letters from those who were preparing to take the
same step, or were at least troubled in spirit.   "It is not
easy to answer," he wrote one who asked for advice, "I
might say that you should not be influenced by the various
personalities that God flings across the orbit of our progress through space.   We have to choose the personalities we shall cling to.   In that we differ from the planets.
But the choice must be yours aided by divine grace.   And
you cannot be a good Christian without patience any
more than you can without charity or humility."

While Selden Delany was at the Beda several important converts came there from other lands.   Vernon

Johnson, whose life paralleled that of Dr. Delany in many ways, came from England to prepare for the priesthood, and Dr. Orchard of England and Mar Ivanos, the convert from the Indian Jacobite schismatic church, came to visit.

Selden Delany had spent three busy happy years in Rome, and had already received the tonsure and minor orders when his health began to trouble him. No doubt those years had been a heavy drain on him, for he was already fifty-six years old when he left New York. The use of his right hand became impaired and the trouble grew worse in spite of treatment, until finally he could hardly write. A specialist in Rome examined him and gave a verdict which made it necessary to proceed immediately with his ordination. He was told he had a rare disease, a form of muscular paralysis which, since it was spinal in nature, as a rule ended fatally.

As he faced his future his buoyant spirits failed him for the first time. He spent a short time in the Blue Nuns' hospital and then in retreat preparatory to his ordination, meantime practising in the Beda chapel the ceremonies of the Mass. To Joseph McNulty, the English student who was his especial friend, he confided his fears that he would never be ordained or ever say Mass. But on St. Patrick's day, in the white and gold vestments sent him a few months before by a former parishioner of St. Mary's in New York, he reached the goal of his desire and was ordained priest in the Lateran Seminary.

Now he felt better in health and spirit. He decided to go home as soon as possible and get medical advice.

After a farewell audience with the Holy Father, who had watched his course at the Beda with sympathetic interest and who gave him a large medal of St. John the Baptist, and after affectionate goodbyes to the men he had been associated with for four years, he sailed for America, hopeful that the disease could be arrested by specialists and that he would still be of some use to the Church in the United States. For a time it seemed that he would. With only slight difficulty he sang a High Mass at the church of Our Lady of Lourdes where he had been received into the Church four years before. Afterwards he was moved to tears at the sight of many of his old friends waiting in the crowd before the church to welcome him home, some of them Catholics now, some still in the other fold.

During the months that followed he was able to carry out some activities; he spoke at various meetings and occasionally he accepted some of the many invitations showered on him. One evening he was dining at the Harvard Club when three of his former classmates joined him at dinner. "But how about this — don't you object to dining with heretics like this?" one asked. The old twinkle was in his eyes. "I certainly do not. There is very good precedent for eating with sinners."

But his health did not return, and Cardinal Hayes, who had hoped to give him the rectorship of a city church, was obliged to give him a simpler charge. He sent him to the Convent of Jesus and Mary at Highland Mills, to be chaplain there. It was a lovely spot, high in the Ramapo

Hills, where in the mornings he celebrated Mass, gave communion to the nuns, and spent the rest of the day writing the book which was to be the answer to *Why Rome?* The Sisters were devoted to him and aided him in every way. One of them acted as his typist and took dictation for him, for he could no longer use his right arm except for signing, very carefully and very painfully, his initials to the letters she typed for him. When the whole right arm became weaker others of the Sisters contrived arrangements of ribbons of the feast or feria color to tie around his arm so that in saying the Mass he could hold the paten more surely. Before long even that loving attempt had to be adjudged unwise. He managed to say the Midnight Mass on Christmas, 1934, but it was almost his last. In February, he wrote Father McNulty from St. Elizabeth's hospital in New York about his wish to have a *cafe latte* with him and to watch the sunset view from the Pincio. "But I have long since," he added, "given up the idea of afternoon tea. And it is more likely that my next view will be from the ramparts of Heaven, should I ever arrive there."

In March he spoke at a communion breakfast, but the disease had progressed so far that he now found it almost impossible to hold up his head unless it was supported. He died on July 5, 1935, and was buried at his own request in the nuns' little cemetery at Highland Mills, in the shadow of a great crucifix. Here the Sisters who had given him such loving care could come to say prayers for him, and his friends could join them at least in spirit to ask the help and prayers of a man who had sought God all the days of his life and had never rested until the search was ended.

Dr. Delany's conversion was important for two reasons : first, because of the outstanding position he had held for years in the Anglican communion ; the second reason was the course that his spiritual pilgrimage took : his invincible determination to follow where God meant him to go ; his decision to leave the road he had walked so long and where so many depended on him to help them over the rough places, to go a lonely way, a greatly daring way, no longer the leader but the led ; and, last of all, his patience when, after his dream of serving God by offering Him daily in the Sacrifice of the Mass, had been attained, he saw the dream that had become fact, fade after a few months to a dream again.

He learned that he must serve another way — a very hard way for a man of his energy and force, a man whose whole life had been one of activity. Those who were with him during his last difficult months agreed that he never complained, that when someone entered his room he always turned his head with a smile on his face, and that, though the hand could scarcely press his visitor's hand at the last, even that slight pressure made plain the friendly sincerity that shone from his eyes.

The visitors who came to see him that last spring of his life, as he lay on his hospital bed, his mind alert as ever, though the hands that ached to serve his Lord lay useless, were witnesses that God had found something for him to do after his brief turn as an active priest was over. So many came that sometimes the nurses feared he would be worn out, but he wanted them all to come. And though he had been renowned in his former church for his clear persuasive voice, and that voice could now scarcely be understood, there was much more to hear in these difficult broken utterances than there had been in the fluent eloquence of former years.

One of his outstanding characteristics was a receptive spirit. He would listen carefully and courteously to anyone who sought his advice but when the advice came it was straight and outspoken, a thing which often annoyed those who, as he complained, "talked so much and said so little." He was always anxious to listen to a real problem and help solve it. And, when his own problem became overwhelming, he took it straight to God and listened for the answer. When that answer came, he put behind him the life he had enjoyed, the financial ease, the good opinion of the many who felt he had betrayed them, for intensive study in a distant land, allowing his days and ways to be completely changed, allowing himself who had been the guide to become the guided. He faced in a strange land possible loneliness, possible poverty, and, as it happened, illness and incapacity just when four years of hard work had made him feel he was at last ready to serve God.

To a friend who, more than once struggled with grief and a certain indignation at the sight of this seeming negation of the hard work of four long years, he would say warningly, for he caught her look, "God has been very good to me." And God was very good too to the old friends and the new brought to his bedside by his fatal illness. Those who came into his room had the opportunity to see how a true Christian takes death merely as a part of life, as the opening of a door and not its closing.

From the day he became a Catholic he was completely one, in his humility, his willingness, his abandonment to God. When his fatal illness was already manifesting itself, he wrote, "If God needs me for any further work in this world He will take care of me. If not He will take me to a better world. I have never had a moment's regret for the change I have made. I feel now that I am buoyed up by a worthwhile institution worthy of the best I can give and I have nothing to apologize for and nothing to fear."

# BIBLIOGRAPHY

Brownson, H. F. : *Brownson's Early Life.* H. F. Brownson, 1898.

Coleman, Caryl : A *Forgotten Convert. Catholic World,* 1925.

Delany, Selden Peabody : *Why Rome?* Dial Press, 1930.

Dutton, Charles : *Samaritans of Molokai.* Dodd, Mead, 1932.

Elliott, Walter : *Life of Father Hecker.* Columbus Press, 1894.

Farmer, Wilmoth A. : A *Missionary Heroine of Kuang-Si.* Foote and Davis, Atlanta, 1912.

Gillis, James M. : *The Paulists.* Macmillan, 1932.

Heagney, H. J. : *Blockade Runner.* Longmans, Green, 1939.

Hecker, Isaac T. : *The Church and the Age.* Paulist Press.

Hewit, Augustine F. : *Memoir of Francis A. Baker.* Columbus Press, 1865.

Lathrop, Rose Hawthorne : *Memories of Hawthorne.* Houghton, Mifflin, 1897.

*Life of Cornelia Connolly* by a Religious of the Society. Longmans, Green, 1938.

McAllister, Anna Shannon : *In Winter We Flourish.* Longmans, Green, 1939.

O'Grady, John : *Levi Silliman Ives.* Kenedy, 1933.

Pine, M. S. : *John Bannister Tabb.* Georgetown Visitation Convent, 1915.

Russell, E. H. : *Correspondence between Thoreau and Hecker. Atlantic Monthly,* 1902.

Sargent, Daniel : *Four Independents.* Sheed and Ward, 1935.

Shuster, George : *Father Tabb and the Romantic Tradition.*
     *The Month,* 1924.

Stone, James Kent : *An Awakening and What Followed.*
     Ave Maria Press.

Swift, Lindsay : *Brook Farm.*   Macmillan, 1904.

Tabb, M. Jannie : *Father Tabb.*   Stratford, 1921.

Walworth, Clarence : *Oxford Movement in America.*   Columbus Press, 1925.


*Periodicals:*

The American Catholic Historical Society Records.

The Ave Maria.

The Bede Review, Rome, 1935.

The Catholic World.

The Commonweal.

The Epistle.

The Lamp.

The Missionary.

The New York Times, 1935.

The Vermonter.

The World-Telegram.